COUNTRY TOWNS OF

New Mexico

COUNTRY TOWNS OF

New Mexico

by Kathryn Gabriel

Country Roads Press
Oaks, Pennsylvania

Country Towns of New Mexico
© 1996 by Kathryn Gabriel. All rights reserved.

Published by Country Roads Press
P.O. Box 838, 2170 West Drive
Oaks, Pennsylvania 19456

Cover design by Caroline Hagen
Cover © 1996 illustration by Michael McCurdy
Photographs © 1996 by Kathryn and Andrew Gabriel
Typesetting by Free Hand Press.

ISBN 1-56626-168-6
Library of Congress
Cataloging-in-Publication Data

Gabriel, Kathryn
    Country Towns of New Mexico / Kathryn Gabriel.
        p.   cm.
    Includes bibliographical references and index
    ISBN 1-56626-168-6 (alk. paper)

    1. New Mexico-Guidebooks. 2. Cities and towns-New
Mexico-Guidebooks. 3. Country life-New Mexico. I. Title.
F794.3.G33 1996
917.8904'53—dc21   96-47899
                                                         CIP

Special Sales

Bulk purchases of Country Roads Press guides are available to corporations at
special discounts. The Special Sales Department can produce custom editions to
be used as premiums and/or for sales promotion to suit individual needs. Existing
editions can be produced with custom cover imprints such as corporate logos. For
more information write to: Special Sales, Country Roads Press, P.O. Box 838,
Oaks, PA 19456

Printed in Canada.
10 9 8 7 6 5 4 3 2 1

For the following New Mexicophiles: Bob, Alice, Janet, Randy, Patty, Jessica, Matt, Saundra, Kaitlin, Jacob, and Andrew Gabriel; David, Cal, and Vangie Loving; and Brandy DeArmond.

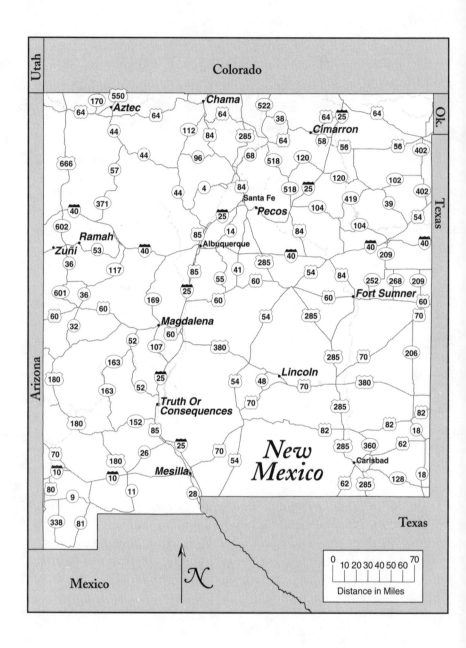

CONTENTS

Introduction IX

1 Aztec 1

2 Chama 15

3 Ramah 29

4 Zuñi 43

5 Magdalena 53

6 Truth or Consequences 67

7 Mesilla 81

8 Lincoln 97

9 Pecos 111

10 Cimarron 127

11 Fort Sumner 141

Bibliography 157

Index 161

INTRODUCTION

The West is still untamed in rural New Mexico. Despite what Santa Fe shop owners might have you believe, no turquoise coyotes bay at pink moons on blue mesas; no shellacked rattlers slither through seas of sage and saltbush; no metallic hunchbacked flute players serenade tourists. This is New Mexico, where the antelope really do play on the plains against sierra vistas, where cows apathetically stroll out in front of traffic, and where one, rather unpleasantly, sweats mud.

The true enchantment of New Mexico's country towns is the historical interplay between Pueblo, Navajo, Apache, Mexican, and European influences, resulting in a unique architectural, artistic, and culinary blend. But these towns have ridden out the jack rabbit and burro cycles of prosperity. They have felt the brunt of the Spanish Conquest, the Mexican War, American expansionism, land wars, and, yes, even the Civil War. The glorious and brutal past of New Mexico continues to sculpt the character of her towns today.

Yesterday in small town New Mexico emanates from those who did not abandon it. For many of the backbone citizens whose ancestors opened the frontier, the edge between getting by and not is still rather thin. Opinions run strong and conservative, though no town is without its vanguard of visionaries. One's genealogical heritage, as bittersweet as it may be, provides continuity, and for some, the past constitutes an avocation, a living, even an obsession. But not all residents are natives. Many are big-city refugees who answered an inaudible call to be our cultural custodians, and they've filled in the gap with their financial backing and drive. The stigma of being a newcomer demands tenacity, yet when you get right down to it, we are all newcomers to this land.

I am a native New Mexican, born and raised in Albuquerque, a metropolis by contrast and light years away from places like Ramah and Fort Sumner. The small towns of my state, however, are the stars on my flag, the constellations by which I navigate. They are not foreign to me, yet I will always be a stranger to them.

My parents were not natives, but they became New Mexicophiles at an early age. My mother, Alice, moved here from Texas at twenty-one on a simple invitation from a friend. She stayed. My father, Bob, arrived a decade or so earlier from Illinois because his tubercular father, Frank, needed the services of the cottage industry of pre-World War II New Mexico. (Frank Gabriel became administrator of Presbyterian, one of the state's first tuberculosis hospitals.) Dad's clientele later included the Navajo Reservation and a couple of governors. Business trips turned into sightseeing ventures; my childhood was strangely illustrated with slide shows of desolate buttes shot through the windshield and one governor's hunting trophy room.

Being the first-born, I was often brought along with the camera bag. Family lore has it that as an infant I sat on the edge of an 800-foot cliff on the reservation cramming rocks into my cheeks. Navajo women, thinking I was an albino, rubbed my blonde hair, supposedly for luck. In later years, we—now including a sister, Janet, and two brothers, Randy and Matt—sought out Indian ruins, ghost towns, and Mexican cuisine in sprawling adobe haciendas. The third seat of the Mercury station wagon faced backwards; whoever sat there and could withstand the carsickness saw much of New Mexico in retrospect—as I still see it.

Perhaps not surprisingly, my initial instinct as a writer has always been to explore the First Peoples of New Mexico, who for thousands of years constructed their homes directly from the earth. Despite the huge passage of time, seemingly disparate cultural groups have tended to build their towns on top of the old villages. When cutting a core sample through the state's Rock of Ages, people, places, and events consequently appear as if layered upon one another like the alternating strata of red and yellow sandstone, black coal deposits, and white-gray ash of the Four Corners where New Mexico squares up with Arizona, Colorado, and Utah.

New Mexico is the fifth largest state in the union, yet it represents only one percent of the country's total population. There's room for one person every thirteen miles or so, and that's probably a good thing. Some seventy towns, villages, and hamlets, not including Pueblos, have a population of under six thousand, thereby meeting the criteria for inclusion in this book and making the selection process painfully difficult. Many best-known towns were regrettably omitted, not because of their unworthiness, but because the entire state and its multiple layers of history and culture had to be represented by a cross section. Towns that made the cut presented multiple layers of history, points of interest, and accommodations. Truth or Consequences, now boasting an estimated seventy-five hundred, was included as a slice of New Mexico's quirkiness. Zuñi is the other exception, also at seventy-five hundred, as the state's only Indian reservation that looks like a modern town. No single town, however, lives in such isolation that they can be discussed apart from the context of the towns that connect to them historically, culturally, and economically.

New Mexico is a system of ancient and historic trails: El Camino Real, the Long Walk, the Santa Fe Trail, the Goodnight-Loving Trail, the Butterfield Overland, the Billy the Kid Trail, Route 66, and Jornada del Muerto (Route of the Dead Man) to name a few and not to mention numerous railroad spurs, branches, and thoroughfares. These trails cross a variety of land forms divided into four major regions, all of which extend beyond political borders: the Rocky Mountains, the Colorado Plateau, the Great Plains, and the Basin and Range Province. In *Country Towns of New Mexico*, you'll meet some of the explorers and outlaws who blazed these trails and forged the towns that stud them.

You will also meet the steamers, puffers, and historical custodians of these towns: the great granddaughter of the man who defended Billy the Kid in Old Mesilla; descendants of the Ramah Mormons who escaped Pancho Villa; a Buffalo Soldier offspring in Lincolntown; a Navajo playwright at Aztec; the cowboy muralists of Fort Sumner and a Pueblo Indian muralist at a Zuñi mission. You'll tour the old jail of Cimarron with only a flashlight, sit in Geronimo's personal hot springs at Truth or Consequences, and spend the night in Chama's Prohibition-era (and still precarious) hotel across the street from a narrow-gauge train depot. You'll go on a rare tour of the Forked Lightning Ranch in Pecos, which is the site of an ancient Indian trade fair, a stage stop on the Santa Fe Trail, a Union camp during a Civil War battle, a dude ranch for rodeo promoter Tex Austin, and home to the late Oscar-winner Greer Garson rolled into one. You'll meet a bevy of people who operate inns, restaurants, shops, and acreage where Billy the Kid slept, ate, was brought to trial, caught, and, eventually, shot. You might even find a metallic hunchbacked flute player or pink coyote in the many shops and galleries. There will be various switchbacks in dates, people, and history as we move from town to town.

New Mexico has always maintained its own balance. Something about the land allows for temporary prosperity or legend but rarely tolerates arrogance for too long. It is from the earth that reputations and empires are built, and it is to the earth they return. Any man or woman who has dared crack the whip of industry has also felt the sting of its business end. Small towns wax and wane in a paradox of their own making. They strive for preservation, yet their sustenance and revitalization come from embracing the fresh visions of newcomers.

New Mexico is famous for its *este es su casa* cordiality and its leisure attitude toward time, especially in the rural areas. The stereotype can be unsettling for visitors used to a more hectic pace, but time's passage depends on one's point of view. Despite its bold landscapes, New Mexico is a land of subtleties, and it takes time to notice all of the detail. Except in two or three of the larger towns, New Mexicans don't honk their horns to unclog a parade of "low-rider" cars or to speed up a tractor. Furthermore, *poco tiempo* or slow time does not connote backwardness—everyone here has the same access to network television, cable, and the Internet as anywhere else. Though country folks do have busy schedules, no one is too busy to spare a few moments with a stranger. They'll even impart a good scandal, especially one that has already sustained decades of speculation. But gossip is a commodity. One must be willing to adhere to the exchange system and be prepared to pay with time, agreement, purchase, or taking comments off the record or, as the case may be, on the record.

So much of the history in these country towns is by word of mouth, and dates, events, and place names often contradict each other or become confused and are then published erroneously. I tried to untangle the knots wherever I could, and I take full responsibility for mistakes. The result has been that within these pages some of the towns are accurately and fully documented for the first time. I'd like to thank the following people not already mentioned in the chapters for their time, interest, help, and trust: Deah Folk of the Aztec Pioneer Museum, Virginia Lattie of the Aztec Chamber of Commerce, the rangers at Aztec Ruins National Monument, Johanna Hartwig of Ramah, Pat O'Hanlon of the Truth or Consequences Public Library, Fermin Salas of the El Morro National Monument, Linda Pabletich of the Cimarron Inn and RV Park, and Connie Beil of Blue Moon Eclectics in Cimarron.

In researching this book, I passed the tradition of seeking New Mexico on to my thirteen-year-old son, Andrew, also a native. As gofer and caddie, he snapped pictures, endured long-winded interviews on sweltering afternoons, worked up a casual interest in what he termed "special dead people," and grew another inch. We visited eleven towns in as many days, logging more than two thousand miles. I thought I'd be revisiting my childhood; instead, I discovered a New Mexico I never knew existed.

Directions:

The town lies at the junction of U.S. Route 550, New Mexico Route 574, and New Mexico Route 44 in the northeast corner of New Mexico. The Aztec Ruins National Monument is northwest of the intersection on U.S. Route 550. Population: 5,479; elevation: 5,644; county: San Juan.

Highlights:

Prehistoric Native American ruins and pioneer-era log buildings; the quality waters of the San Juan River; early railroads and depots; adobes built by Civil War veterans; J.T. Green's Opera House; Miss Gail's Inn; Pioneer Village; Chaco Canyon and Mesa Verde; the annual Anasazi Pageant; the four-hundred-room Animas River People's great house, A.D. 1111 to 1115.

CHAPTER 1

AZTEC

The Tree Rings of Aztec

he rings on the old tree that is Aztec reveal an array of distinctive eras. The shady red-brick façades along Main present a Midwestern aura despite the pyramid images the name conjures up. Individualized houses in the historic district are reminders of more genteel eras characterized by George, Anne, and Victoria. At the north end of Main is a life-size village of authentic homesteads where pioneer-era log buildings line up like jars of preserves in the cellar. Just to the northwest are the remnants of a prehistoric sandstone palace enveloped by relatively modern neighborhoods and farms. For more than a century, the citizens of Aztec have creatively braided the different cultural and architectural branches of their orchards into an aesthetic and, more importantly, functional basket.

The chief characteristic of San Juan County, of which Aztec has been the seat since 1887, is its immense water supply, greater than that of the rest of the state. The "quality waters" of the San Juan River, rated third in the world for fly fishing, are just eighteen miles east of Aztec. Nearby Navajo Lake has two hundred miles of shoreline. Stock raisers from Colorado, Texas, and southern New Mexico found the grassy mesas and valleys appealing when it was thrown open to settlers in the late 1870s. But the rich soil, reddish in tint, along with a good climate proved to be ideal for farming, particularly fruit. By the end of the century, the area was populated by Midwestern farmers and Civil War veterans. The same conditions no doubt prompted the prehistoric farmers, called the Anasazi, to build their communities along the Animas River nearly a thousand years earlier.

Informally, this was Navajo country. Nomadic by lifestyle, the Navajos were not the ones who built the sandstone cities, but arrived in the sixteenth century long after the cities were abandoned. They may have hidden from their enemies in the ruins they call *Kin Keel* (with various spellings), but the name was never adopted by the white settlers. Spanish friars in search of a shorter route to California noted the ancient ruins on their map in 1776. They named the nearby river *Los Animas de los Perditos*, River of the Lost Souls. One story is that when the Spanish fought the Indians in the Animas Valley, they considered their unbaptized souls to be damned and tossed the dead bodies into the river. The river, nevertheless, claimed the souls of many Indians and explorers alike who tried to cross its treacherous waters. The trail through the valley was used by the Spanish for many years, but the area remained fairly unblemished by Navajo-fearing outsiders during the 1800s, except for the occasional gold seekers, trappers, and military reconnoiters.

In 1862, the U.S. Army sent General Christopher "Kit" Carson to remove the Navajos to a reservation at Bosque Redondo on the Pecos River under the guard of Fort Sumner. (See Fort Sumner chapter.) An 1868 treaty returned them to their homelands bordering the Aztec area. The only other consideration holding back the tide of settlers were the Jicarilla Apaches, who had also been held prisoners of war with their linguistic cousins and enemies at Fort Sumner. The Apaches rejected the reservation granted them in 1874 in the eastern portion of the county because it was too close to the Navajos. This opened up the area to squatting in 1876 and homesteading in 1878.

One of the primary pioneer families in the area were the Blancetts— first headstones on the right in the Aztec cemetery. "There's more of them up there than walking around," said Tweeti Blancett, wife of Linn Blancett, who is a descendant of Marcellus ("Cell") Blancett. Cell had scouted the area for the U.S. Army in the early 1870s and by the end of the decade, the entire Blancett clan had migrated from Colorado. Cell and his father, Moses, cleared one hundred and sixty acres of homestead land south of Aztec for running cattle and dug an irrigation ditch using only hand tools. A number of Blancett men served as sheriffs in the area and were instrumental in forming the fabric of the Aztec community. A number of them also met with violent deaths in their early ages, and it was left to the women to forge the Blancett dynasty.

Northern New Mexico had been settled by many Hispanics during the Spanish and Mexican reigns prior to U.S. takeover in 1846. Some military personnel were granted acreage as reward while others, who accompanied the Conquistadors as support staff, settled virgin lands and homesteaded when the law provided for it. The Archuleta family, among the latter, had come to the region in 1872. Cell Blancett's uncle, John, was allegedly shot in the back in 1882 by Guadalupe Archuleta. One story is that John was serving papers on Archuleta for stealing sheep when he was shot and "if this is true, one wonders why he turned his back on him," says Tweeti. The other story is that Blancett was shot for fooling around with Archuleta women and "if that's true, I can see why he was shot in the back." The dispute was most likely over fence boundaries, she added. John's brother, Moses, appointed by the Territorial governor as head of the militia, hung Archuleta without a trial. "Justice was swift in those days and we can't judge it by today's standards."

Tweeti, formerly Triciafaye Walser of Alamagordo, New Mexico, and formerly a state representative and city manager, built a motor lodge called the Step Back Inn at the main intersection of town. Each of the forty rooms is named for a Hispanic or Anglo pioneer family who homesteaded the area between 1872 and the 1890s. Decorated with turn-of-the-century furnishings, the spacious rooms lack no modern conveniences. There are telephones, recliners, and blow dryers in every room, and television sets are hidden inside every chiffonnier.

The original homesteader of the townsite was John Koontz from Pennsylvania. Koontz knew what he was doing, having gained experience in laying out portions of Omaha and Fremon, Nebraska, and Denver, Colorado. His considerable holdings included the ancient ruins. He lived on the corner of Chaco and Park Avenues where the auditorium now sits and ran a general store and stagecoach stop in a one-room flat-roofed adobe. In 1878, the territory established a post office in Koontz's store. In 1890, he sold forty acres to the Aztec Town

Company and later sold at least another hundred and sixty acres to other individuals before moving to California, although he did donate a lot for the Presbyterian church. The board initially plotted some two hundred and forty acres and sold lots to citizens for home and business sites.

The town really didn't take off until the Red Apple Flyer, a wide-gauge branch of the otherwise narrow-gauge Denver and Rio Grande, Western Railroad, arrived in 1905, thereby connecting Farmington to Durango. You can see the 1905 depot, now addressed as 408 North Rio Grande, on the northeast edge of the historic district. Though the rails and ties have been removed and the station remodeled into a residence, it remains as an important reminder of the pivotal role the railroad played in the town's history. Indeed, the introduction in the 1870s and 1880s of the industry revolutionized New Mexico.

The Red Apple Flyer ran a regular six-days-per-week schedule, expressing San Juan fruit, beans, hay, and livestock to northern markets in exchange for Midwestern families, architecture, and agricultural values, at a speed of fifteen to eighteen miles per hour. In August, 1923, the Red Apple Flyer went narrow gauge. When it pulled out on a Friday for Durango, five hundred men went to work to change the rails, and by Monday, the new narrow gauge left on schedule from Durango back to the San Juan. A caboose from the old D&RGW at Chama was acquired by former State Senator Ray Atchison and moved to the Pioneer Village. Leather seats and a potbelly stove grace its interior.

Meanwhile, the Territory of New Mexico legislature established Aztec temporarily as the seat of the newly created San Juan County in 1887. A number of communities protested and in 1890, Junction City won a close election for the seat with Aztec coming in second and Farmington receiving a single vote. County officials in Aztec refused to budge until they received court orders, but in the meantime, Junction City never provided a building. Finally, the Territorial Supreme Court decided in favor of Aztec in 1892. Farmington helped fund the building of a two-story brick courthouse in Aztec in 1898, but the issue continued to be a hot topic of debate for another half a century at ballgames and elections.

Aztec ruins right in the middle of Aztec town.

A bit of that infamous stubbornness is still alive in Aztec today, and it is characterized by the architecture that has resisted modernization. A walking-tour brochure, available at various sites (somewhat confusingly), directs sightseers to twenty-four buildings on Main, eleven of which are on the National Register of Historic Places and the New Mexico State Register of Cultural Properties. An additional sixty-seven structures in the residential area are also registered.

One of the oldest buildings in Aztec is the General Store at 101 South Main, first built in 1890 by Civil War veteran Colonel W. H. Williams. It was made of adobe brick and originally faced east with a roof over the sidewalk. It was remodeled with a brick coat in 1919 to house the Aztec State Bank, which was taken over by the Citizens Bank in 1930. Colonel Williams was the trustee of the Aztec Town Company and the president of Citizens Bank.

The founder of Citizens was T.A. Pierce who moved here in 1903 with his family and an iron safe which constituted the beginnings of the bank first located at 101 North Main. By 1905, the bank moved to 105 South Main, and an exact replica of the original bank was built at the Pioneer Village at the museum by Pierce descendants at a cost of $25,000. It houses the teller's windows and other furnishings from the original building. The building at 101 North Main became J.T. Green's Opera House (Green was Aztec's first mayor), and apparently the present building on this corner looks remarkably like the original. This structure also housed the first picture show, called the Star Theater. The Pierce Mansion, at 202 North Mesa Verde, is described as a Georgian Revival, Prairie Style. It was built in 1906 in the middle of a half-acre lot and was the first to install indoor plumbing. He could afford it.

We stayed at Miss Gail's Inn, a bed and breakfast and one of the registered buildings on Main. Best night's sleep I'd had in months, despite the fact that Main is also the highway. In the evening, I sat out on the porch swing and watched an old man shuffle down to the gas station for a soda and then shuffle home—a journey that took about twenty minutes. Gail and John Aspromonte bought the 1907 hotel a few years ago and refurbished each of the ten rooms in country wallpapers, panelling, and quilts; two have kitchenettes. Gail plans a gift shop in the basement to sell her own handmade quilts.

Miss Gail's was originally the American Hotel, built to accommodate the increased population brought in by the railroad. The kiln-fired bricks are older than the building. Hotel operators fetched guests from the depot in a horse-drawn wagon and in the beginning rented out cots to people who just needed to rest for a few hours. The hotel hosted many weddings, housed the famous restaurant operated by Hattie Lair, and supposedly installed the first telephone. The Lairs lived in the adjoining cottage built in 1878. As with all old buildings, there's some talk of ghosts: a wedding couple most often sighted in Room 5. (We didn't see them.) Gail's theory is that the ghosts originated from the earlier 1888 schoolhouse that had once been used as a church where the hotel now stands. The business continued as the Aztec Residential Hotel until the Aspromontes bought it a few years ago.

Unwittingly, I started a domino effect of phone calls down Main Street when I mentioned that the brochures of both Miss Gail's and the Step Back Inn claimed to have had some connection with being the first hotel built in Aztec. According to the "Step Back To Aztec's Roots" brochure, Tweeti's deceased in-law, Mrs. Moses Blancett, otherwise known as Grandmother "Monie," ran a hotel in Aztec until 1908. Rent was two dollars a week; board, two bits a meal. The director of the museum hurriedly searched through some books and discovered no beginning date for Monie's hotel, and so no conclusion could be made about whether or not it beat the 1907 date of the American Hotel. However, the first hotel, according to Aztec's walking tour, was built at 112 North Main and run by an English character named Jarvis between 1890 and 1903, when he died.

In the early 1900s, Aztec citizens built their residences between Main and the Lower Animas Irrigation Ditch where the depot sits. Built in 1878, narrow feeders of the irrigation system still cross many of the front yards as a thread of continuity between the neighborhood and its past. Terms such as hipped cottage, free classic, and simplified Anne are used to describe most of the homes, cottages, and bungalows.

The G.W. McCoys may have been the first to replace their log cabin when they erected the brick house at 901 North Rio Grande, and it may have been one of the best of the local hipped cottages. The original forty-acre orchard has dwindled to one apple tree standing near the house. The town likes to call attention to the Eblen-Case and Bunker-Beaver houses, both built in 1907 on North Mesa Verde. The former is unique for its excellent state of preservation, shingled exterior walls on the second story, and an octagonal tower on the northeast corner. The latter house was built by Fred Bunker who developed Lovers Lane which was first named after him. The five houses on Lovers Lane "would have made an impressive approach to the town from the depot."

The people of Aztec are visually oriented. They like to have their history out where they can see it, walk through it, and touch it. Merle Pinkerton, a retired oil-field worker, came up with the idea of displaying the museum's stockpiles of antiques in their natural surroundings. Besides the bank replica and the caboose, the Pioneer Village includes Aztec's original jail as well as a doctor's office, sheriff's office, magistrate office, general store, post office, blacksmith and harness shop, and school, all reconstructed from original buildings in the area. Tucked discreetly in the back of the village, there's even a two-seater outhouse wreathed in authentic spider webs.

The Hamblett log cabin was moved in from the Three-H spread near Farmington. The one-room cabin was so tiny, the men had to draw numbers to see who could dance with the women inside while the others smoked and chewed tobacco out in the cold. In 1880, the Porter Stockton Gang, formerly of the Allison Gang, got a little drunk and crashed a Christmas Eve party in this cabin with pistols firing. Two men were shot. Stockton was later killed by a posse and lies in a shallow grave somewhere between Farmington and Aztec.

The 1906 church is from Cedar Hill eleven miles north of Aztec. It was too tall to be trucked down the highway, so it was completely dismantled and rebuilt on the lot. The pews, pulpit, chairs, piano and stool, hymn book, and Bible are all original contents. Weddings and other celebrations are still held in the church.

Visitors can see how Aztec took on newer and newer technology like so many layers of clothing by walking through the nearby Pioneer Museum collections. There's a barber shop set up to take customers, a costume room, an agricultural room, a telephone room, and an office and clock room filled with antique equipment. The Lobato Room is a collection of collections: sea shells, fossils, rocks, old glass, arrowheads, and prehistoric Indian artifacts. It also contains wool and sheep-shearing equipment, perhaps representing the traditional family business. Out back are wagons, buggies, sleighs, oxen yokes, plows, and farm machinery.

An important display is the 1920 Fort Worth Spudder Drilling Rig with its wooden derrick reaching for the sky, "just like those early wild catters who made it work" boasts the literature. On display is the old "dog house," oilman's office furnished with log books, tools, and obligatory coffee pot. Equipment from Project Gasbuggy, used in the first underground nuclear explosion for oil and gas exploration in 1967, is also exhibited.

Although testing for oil began in the San Juan Basin as early as 1901, showings were skimpy or financially problematic to extract. A third local company, the Aztec Oil Syndicate, drilled a well on the outskirts of South Aztec in 1921 and found a large flow of gas at 985 feet and oil at 1750 feet. The gas was piped to Aztec, and the town became the first in the state to use natural gas for domestic purposes. Shallow fields were left open, and at night, people lit the gas for their private gatherings. The company went broke, however, and the system was sold to individuals. This opened the field to such companies as Southern Union Gas, Continental Oil, and Santa Fe Oil Company. The San Juan Basin has rich coal and oil deposits, and the national need for new resources in the 1970s revitalized the region's economy.

The final segment of the Aztec saga concerns her first citizens. The ruins intrigued the early pioneers, particularly the Howes, who moved from Pennsylvania into a little log cabin a mile north of the ruins in 1880. At age eleven or twelve, Sherman Howe accompanied his teacher, John Johnson, and other students in the first exploration of the Aztec ruins during the winter of 1881-82, although it had also been previously studied by a geologist and an anthropologist. Howe devoted every spare minute of his life to the study and exploration of the ruins. In 1916, the American Museum of Natural History began sponsoring excavations, spearheaded by the twenty-five-year-old archaeologist, Earl Morris, and seven years later, the ruins became a national monument.

The original settlers were not too unlike their successors. Beginning in A.D. 100, they built several hundred farming communities along the Animas and San Juan Rivers. Their first structures were pits in the ground covered with roofs of branches and mud. Eventually, they built above-ground single- and double-story rows of rooms near their former pit houses, called *pueblos* or villages. They traded with similar communities that sprang up in other drainages and terraces across the Colorado Plateau covering an area where New Mexico, Colorado, Utah, and Arizona join together at their four corners. Today, the people are known collectively as the Anasazi (Ah-nah-saw´zee), a Navajo word for ancient enemy or the ancient ones, depending how it is pronounced.

Sometime during the tenth century A.D., the Anasazi began turning their modest pueblos into monumental sandstone complexes. The massive walls consisted of dressed sandstone exteriors sandwiching a core of unshaped stones and mud mortar. These so-called great houses incorporated large, circular, underground chambers called great kivas where the people probably met to dance and perform their religious duties. The model was at Pueblo Bonito in Chaco Canyon, some sixty-five miles due south of the Aztec ruins. Archaeologists perceive Chaco Canyon, with its nine cathedral towns, as the economical or ceremonial hub of a cultural region 26,000 square miles in area. Long, wide boulevards radiated from Chaco Canyon toward outlying towns, and it is believed that the fifty-mile Great North Road may have helped the Animas and San Juan River people, among others, find their way to Chaco and back.

The Animas River people were late bloomers. We know from tree ring and carbon 14 dating that they constructed their great houses between A.D. 1111 and 1115, about the time Chaco's building frenzy slowed to just a few projects, which some archaeologists believe was the result of a shift in political power from Chaco to Aztec. Two great houses at Aztec, pragmatically called the West Ruin and the East Ruin, sit on a rise overlooking the river. About four hundred rooms on three stories, more than two dozen kivas, and a great kiva in the compound comprised the West Ruin. Several hundred people ground corn, skinned small game, made baskets and pottery, traded, and danced here. In 1878, an anthropologist noted that a quarter of the pueblo's stones had been carted away by later Aztec settlers for their homes—a traditional New Mexico practice.

East Ruin remains buried for the improved technology of future generations. A ranger told me that a group of archaeologists, over beers, folded a map of all the ruins into a paper airplane and discovered that the outline of East Ruin is nearly a mirror image of the West Ruin. Like their successors, the Anasazi had a visual acuity and you can bet when you come across a place with a gorgeous view, you're within walking distance of one of their ancient homes.

Aztec Ruins presents a number of other interesting features including structures encased by three walls built up on mounds and near a couple of ancient road segments, but not everything is readily accessible. The great kiva in the central plaza is the only one in the state that has been fully reconstructed and is unusual in that it is above ground. Visitors can enter its cool, quiet depths and imagine the activity that went on in the central fireplaces and the man-size niches in the mezzanine, of sorts. Wide-angle lens a must! It is also fun to duck through the long corridor of rooms on the north wall of the great house and view its inner sanctums through Plexiglas windows placed by park rangers.

When Chaco Canyon was abandoned around A.D. 1130, from drastic politics or weather (the region is not without its long droughts), the system began to collapse. By 1150, activity at Aztec diminished and the villagers trickled away. Then around 1225, the town sprang back, as it did in Chaco Canyon. The pottery, textiles, and other wares of the newcomers are distinctive of Mesa Verde in southern Colorado forty miles to the northwest of Aztec ruins. Mesa Verde is a rugged canyon populated by cliff cities which flourished between A.D. 1200 and 1275. The newcomers remodeled the Animas great houses and built new structures in a style typical of their homeland. Once again, the town thrived and once again, it dwindled away. Thus ended the Anasazi culture as we know it. Descendants may be among any of the nineteen Pueblo groups living in New Mexico today. Their influence will be felt in other towns visited in this book. (See Zuñi chapter.)

We might blame the first Spanish surveyors for associating the ruins with the Aztecs who founded Tenochtitlán (Mexico City) in 1325. The park states unequivocally that the prehistoric builders were not Aztec, although whether or not the Anasazi were influenced or controlled by their contemporaries in Mexico is still being debated in some scientific circles. It is likely the Hispanic settlers sustained the misnomer. William Prescott's immensely popular *Conquest of Mexico*, describing Cortez's annihilation of the Aztec ruler Montezuma (Moctezuma II), began circulating around the time Anglos trickled into the area in the mid-1800s, thereby further promoting the myth of the Aztec origin of the ruins. The town that grew up around the ruins naturally took on the name.

Legislation in 1988 expanded the boundaries of the monument from 27.14 acres to nearly 320 acres, which eventually will include the unexcavated pueblo neighborhoods to the north now on private lands. An issue that generally faces many small towns in New Mexico is striking a balance between preserving ruins and allowing for private enterprise, and the acquisition of the lands north of Aztec Ruin has been a political process.

The turnoff to Chaco Canyon is less than a half hour's drive from Aztec on New Mexico Route 44 to the south, in addition to another thirty miles of dirt road, and requires at least a full day to see. Visitors can either stay in the Aztec-Bloomfield-Farmington area or camp in the park. Mesa Verde is one and a half hours north of Aztec and also requires at least a day to see, although accommodations are more locally accessible. The Aztec monument and its sister Salmon Ruins, near Bloomfield (built around A.D. 1090) just down the road on U.S. Route 64, are not as spectacular, but are geographically and culturally the midpoint between Chaco Canyon and Mesa Verde, and can be toured in an hour or two. Aztec Ruins are one of the most pleasant ruins to visit in the state. In the adjacent river park, you can sit at a picnic table under a cottonwood and view the smooth masonry of the great kiva. One can almost imagine the walls illuminated with the candelit sacks called *farolitos* or *luminarias* the town puts up every Christmas Eve.

When Andrew and I visited Aztec, we saw the Anasazi Pageant at the Lions Wilderness Park Amphitheatre in Farmington. (Take Butler Avenue off U.S. Route 64 or U.S. Route 550 north or Piñon Hills Boulevard northwest and follow the signs to the amphitheater.) Set against the natural sandstone cliffs at sundown, the Anasazi people come alive in the opening scenes of the play that will bring tears to the eyes of students of this culture. The pageant, *Anasazi, the Ancient Ones*, is based on a true story about Sarah Mara Boots, a half Navajo-half Paiute girl who was raised by white settlers after her parents were killed. She was later reclaimed by her Navajo grandmother, Black Shawl, and taught her heritage. When she comes of age, she marries the Mormon missionary, Ira Hatch, and becomes instrumental in releasing the Navajos from their forced reservation at Fort Sumner. Local Navajos make up most of the cast of fifty-two. For an extra cost, playgoers can partake in an excellent plate of barbecue brisket, Anasazi beans, and cobbler. *The Foreigner*, a western comedy by Larry Shue, is also performed at this sight on rotating nights.

Sharon Hatch French, the playwright of *Anasazi the Ancient Ones*, is a descendant of Sarah and played the role of the old Navajo woman to a tee, right down to the earthy sense of humor, high pitched cadence, and waddle. The role of Sarah was written for Sharon's daughter, Julie French Burch, but she played the Mormon woman who raised Sarah when we saw it and now stands in for her mother. Julie owns and operates the Blanco Trading Post on New Mexico Route 44 at one of the dirt roads that leads into Chaco Canyon. She told me she had always wanted to run a trading post, and when this one came up for sale, she convinced her husband to buy it. (His family had been in the business for generations, and it was something he initially resisted.) I spotted some good deals on old pawn jewelry in the case. She now resides in Aztec, and Sharon French sometimes performs at the Salmon Ruins on Friday nights in the summers.

For more information:

(Addresses are in Aztec, NM 87410)
Aztec Museum, Pioneer Village and Oil Field Exhibit, 505-334-9829
Step Back Inn, 505-334-1200
Miss Gail's Inn, 505-334-3452
Aztec's Pioneer Days, 505-334-9551
Tours by Archaeologists, 505-334-6675
Aztec Ruins National Monument, 505-334-6174

Additional information:

Anasazi Pageant, Farmington, NM 87401, 800-448-1240
Salmon Ruin, Bloomfield, NM 87413, 505-632-2013
Chaco Culture National Historic Park,
    Bloomfield, NM 87413, 505-786-7014
Mesa Verde National Park (and area), Cortez, CO 81321, 800-253-1616

Directions:

At the junction of New Mexico Route 17 and U.S. Route 64/84 in north-central New Mexico six miles south of the Colorado state line. Population: 1,048; elevation: 7,850; county: Rio Arriba.

Highlights:

Prohibition's famous Foster's Hotel, with its resident ghosts; the Chama Station Inn and the Shamrock Hotel, both built in the 1930s; prosperity brought by oil pipelines and trains; Jones House B & B, a Tudor-style adobe house; early sheep ranches and their history; Cumbres and Toltec Scenic Railroad; Big Vee's green *chile*.

CHAPTER 2

CHAMA

Sidetracked in Chama

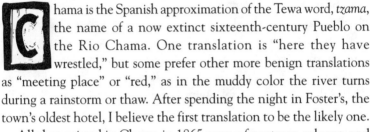hama is the Spanish approximation of the Tewa word, *tzama*, the name of a now extinct sixteenth-century Pueblo on the Rio Chama. One translation is "here they have wrestled," but some prefer other more benign translations as "meeting place" or "red," as in the muddy color the river turns during a rainstorm or thaw. After spending the night in Foster's, the town's oldest hotel, I believe the first translation to be the likely one.

All that existed in Chama in 1865 were a few stores, saloons, and a blacksmith shop. The Denver & Rio Grande, Western Railroad's construction in 1880–81 increased the town's population to a thousand residents. The San Juan extension of the railroad once dipped through Chama, connecting Alamosa-Antonito to Durango-Silverton (all in Colorado) while crossing the border twelve times and covering a total of two hundred and forty-five miles. Today, the Toltec & Cumbres Scenic Railroad still operates a narrow-guage route between Chama and Antonito for train enthusiasts.

The potential for development in this budding railroad town in the 1860s attracted both industrious and disreputable characters alike. Individuals interested in developing the area's coal mines rapidly appeared on the scene and were soon joined by the lumberers, laborers, engineers, and contractors required to build accommodations for the influx. There was no lack of entertainment—saloons, gambling houses, moonshine stills were plenty—but the cost of living was high, as one can well imagine. Opportunistic outlaws like the Charles Allison gang regularly held up the railroad pay car, construction camps with large payrolls, and the recreational establishments. Alas, the period from

1889 until the 1930s was the "greatest era of Chama's history," says the chamber of commerce's literature.

During Prohibition (1920-1933), Chama created a reputation as the moonshine capital of New Mexico, a dubious distinction made possible by the relative isolation of the Chama Valley and the booming of its several industries. None of the villages had local marshalls, and any other official members of the law were invariably on the take. Consequently, all raids by federal agents had to be organized from Santa Fe or Denver. "Revenooer" allies in Santa Fe would telephone Chama magnate T.D. Burns as soon as agents headed out, and by the time they arrived on the near impassable roads—muddy in the summer, snowpacked in the winter—everyone had had enough time to camouflage their stills. By the same token, if agents came in from the north by train, the telegraph operator would initiate the telephone tree. The early-warning system was sort of a community effort because everyone was in the business. "There were so goddamn many of them they had to wear badges to keep from selling it to each other," said one old-timer, making it impossible for understaffed agents to raid every distillery. When agents succeeded in a surprise raid, the irrigation ditches became sewers, and the sight of an occasional tipsy cow was not unusual.

Pivotal to this run-away moonshine town was Foster's Hotel, "the root of all evil," "the headquarters for living, eating, and drinking; mostly drinking," according to the Chama *Tattler*. Built in 1881, Foster's survived several serious fires that gutted the town and is by default the oldest building still standing. Though not the original owner, Henry (a.k.a. Bert) "Pappy" Foster took over the hotel in 1909 or 1910. He was a rough Irishman who peddled a mean moonshine and freely served liquor in his bar during Prohibition. The secret was in not keeping much on hand. Foster would serve it a glass at a time or by the pint and hide the bottles in a dark little room behind the bar equipped with a back door in case a "pro-hi" came around.

The railroad operated a Harvey House restaurant out of the hotel to provide meals for the passengers. Folks would walk up the hill from the train to take a little beverage and perhaps smuggle a bottle home. Buyers for commercial amounts of moonshine arrived on the train and conducted their dealings with a few of the larger operators like Burns over lunch at Foster's. The train also freighted the moonshine out and the raw materials in. One woman remembers watching the mountain men meeting the grain cars and driving their loaded wagons on up the hill. Sugar, corn, and other grains not indigenous to the area are essential ingredients to moonshine, which was called white mule because of its clear color. (Brown sugar discolors whiskey.) One method of distilling liquor was to bury about thirty barrels of mash into the hillside, pack it with manure, and let the warm sunshine do the job.

An old man said when they shipped cattle out of Chama, they slept at Foster's, but when they shipped out sheep, they had to sleep with the stock to protect them from theft. "It used to be hell just to survive." Foster's wasn't too easy to survive, either. Another old man recalled sitting at the bar talking to someone when the lights went out. He regained consciousness in a pool of blood. Doc Dunham picked him up, drove him to his office, and stitched up the cut where the full bottle of beer had struck. Doc advised him to consider the episode part of the initiation process for newcomers to the town and to leave it at that. The identity of the assailant was never discovered.

Dr. J.I. "Doc" Dunham, who had arrived from Tennessee in 1917 and practiced until 1970, was a tough, streetwise character. One time, he called another doctor to join him at Foster's where they would fry up the fine mess of rainbows he had caught. When they sat down to their meal, three or four half-drunk Swedish lumberjacks came in and challenged them to a fight. Doc waded into them with a catsup bottle and dragged them out the door. They shortly returned with a "ham-and-egg" fighter in tow who did not suspect Doc to be hiding behind the door. Upon entering, he met Doc's fist and immediately landed rearwards ten feet away. Later, Doc admitted he knew old man Foster was watching from the kitchen with a Winchester.

Servillia Richards and her liquor-salesman husband Thomas (Pinkie), purchased Foster's in 1946, and Servillia later won it in the divorce settlement from Richards and ran it for thirty years. Servillia's new husband, Warner Johnson, subsequently ran the bar. She had grown up with Foster's daughter Nell, who had run the hotel prior to Servillia's tenure. As a kid, Servillia collected cigar boxes from the bar for crayons and whatnot and in high school went to work in the restaurant washing dishes. Probably one of her more vivid memories was giving birth in the hotel. When she went into labor, Doc was sitting in the bar as usual and she knew he'd be "drunker than a hoot owl," but a county nurse in residence called him up against Servillia's wishes. He staggered into the bathroom to wash his hands and emerged sober enough to deliver the baby.

"Running a bar is the sorriest life a woman ever lived," Servillia said, but it was no more worse than any other bar in the area—and more respectable than most. In 1925, a fire gutted a whole block of Chama just south of Foster's. Legend has it, and this seems to be substantiated by fact, that the good ladies of Chama intentionally set fire to the rooming house next door to the Chama Mercantile because local men had conducted "illicit affairs" with the women who lived, or worked, there. Servillia had heard whisperings of the "den of iniquity" in the boarding house, and she watched the fire from the railyards below, thinking that God was punishing those people for their sins and that the world was coming to an end. The fire leapt to other buildings on the block, but Foster's was spared.

Alice Nuno, the most recent owner of Foster's, told me the rooming house had been torched by Durango ladies who were jealous of the Chama women catering to their men when their train shift brought them to Chama. After the fire, Foster's built an eight-room addition over an apartment to accommodate the customers left homeless by the burning of the two other hotels. Today, the original fourteen rooms of Foster's are condemned, but patrons may still rent one of the later eight rooms. Alice herself restored every room and installed bathrooms and showers.

For three bucks, train passengers can take a shower at Foster's if they want to freshen up, but I must warn you, it takes many minutes for water to reach the upstairs rooms—longer if you prefer it hot. Train buffs, rugged historians, and travelers who don't plan ahead and it's the last room in town may want to try Foster's. It's not fancy and it's not for everyone, but it is clean. We drove into the Chama Valley late one Friday afternoon in July with not a single vacancy sign showing. Foster's, at 393 4th and Terrace, was our last chance. (I missed the Jones House B & B farther north.) Foster's has no formal lobby and despite what the signs say, one registers at the bar. When I asked the bartender if there were any vacancies, she opened the register, ran her hand all the way down an empty page, and said, "Yup." I gave up the only room with two double beds to the family of five who came in on my heels for a room in the front nearest the balcony.

The balcony provides a glorious view of the train-yard activity against the evergreens. The trains constantly whistle and puff and let off steam, all exciting noises by day, but the workers build up the boilers and move the trains all night long as well. Our window opened up to the balcony, and I hoped Andrew's size 10½ shoes in the windowsill would scare off intruders. The bar, boasting live music in the evenings and a pool table, still carries a roughneck aura. (There were more police cars from varying jurisdictions patrolling this town than any other reported in this book.) The restaurant has standard fare including steaks, seafood, sandwiches, and Mexican, and there's a separate dinner theater with reasonable rates in the back of the building. Play titles in the past have appropriately included, *Sidetracked in Chama*, starring Mae Southwest, Willy the Kid, and Justin Time, and *Speak Easy but Dance with a Roar*. The characters come out in costume during train arrivals and departures.

As with all old buildings, this one naturally has its ghosts: A man and a woman haunt the old section. I peeked up there and the place is a wreck, but I didn't see any ghosts. Mrs. Nuno says she's been told she could promote the hotel with the ghost stories, but she's too busy running the place to give it much effort. The hotel business is a lot of hard work.

Two other hotels facing the train yards are the Chama Station Inn and the Shamrock Hotel, both of which come highly recommended. The Chama Station Inn, formerly the Chama Lodge and the Chama Station Lodge, was built circa 1930. The six original rooms have undergone major restoration and have been individually redecorated; two units featuring kiva fireplaces have been added. The outdoor hot tub is a pleasant retreat from a day of cross-country skiing or train tripping.

The Shamrock Hotel opened for business in 1938–39. Lafayette Hughes of Hughes Oil partially funded the hotel's construction, and two rooms were kept for his free and personal use. The décor was supposed to be Spanish–Mediterranean, although it looks more 1930s Southwest-style. Hughes's room was uniquely decorated with a green pedestal sink and a mural of two mermaids on the bathroom wall bearing the words, "don't go fishing."

Lafayette Hughes came to his wealth by marrying Annie Clifton Hughes (same last name, no apparent kin). She was the adopted granddaughter of William Hughes, who left her his 54,000-acre ranch. Together, Annie and Lafayette ran the ranch and 127-acre oil field, named "Gramps" in honor of William, until she died in 1940. The first productive oil well was drilled in 1936, and at the peak in 1942, ten wells were pumping twelve hundred to thirteen hundred barrels of pure oil a day. The 1936 prospectus for Gramps Oil states, "Remember that a knocker never wins and a winner never knocks."

Hughes oil was pumped to Chama through a fifteen-mile sawdust encased pipeline carried on trestles over the canyons and arroyos. It was pumped from a storage tank at the field twenty-four hours a day, about the length of time it took to cross the Continental Divide where gravity siphoned it the rest of the way to a 66,000-barrel storage tank in Chama. It was then pumped through town to a loading rack in the railroad yards where it was loaded into oil tanker cars. The cars held a hundred and fifty barrels of oil, and the train hauled about six to eight cars to the Gramps refinery in Alamosa, Colorado. In cold weather, finned "co-devils" or line cleaners were used to keep the congealing oil from sticking to the sides of the pipe. When the train stopped operating, oil was shipped by truck. By 1986, twenty-six wells were pumping a hundred and thirty barrels a day at Gramps. The glory days of oil, as in all industries of the region, are gone.

The Shamrock was owned and operated by yet another character, Pat Kelly, who lived on the premises until his death in the 1960s. He owned quite a number of businesses in town including a movie the-

Train station in Chama

ater, a bar, and a grocery store in what is now the Cumbres Mall. This adobe complex next to the Shamrock (both on corners of the same street) was extensively renovated into boutiques and gift shops in 1985. The walk-in safe in what is now the deli was used as the bank until a proper bank was built in 1916.

Kelly was literally a lover of wine, women, and song, and his reputation claims that he would proposition any woman within eight hours of her arrival in town. The drunker he got, the better he skated at the roller rink. He operated a distillery at the foot of Rabbit Peak near the Chamita River and sold large quantities of liquor to markets outside of the area through Foster's. A famous practical joker even in boyhood, Kelly and his friend Rip Huntington, who later became a dentist, frequently threw firecrackers into bars, down stovepipes, and onto the stage during performances. One never knew when the firecrackers were dummies or when they would blast the hats off the drinking railroaders and the glasses off the bars. Kelly couldn't take a joke, however.

The Jones House B & B, a 1916 English Tudor-style adobe home, is in the same block as Foster's. It was originally built for the first banker and was purchased in 1940 by Guy Jones who had come from Mississippi to ranch turkeys near what is now El Vado Lake. The turkeys froze in the winter, and he became known as Turkey Jones.

The individual involved in laying out the original town in 1881 was Thomas Catron, who purchased the land from the Martinez family. The town was divided into twenty-five-foot by hundred-foot lots, and buyers could purchase as many lots as they wished. Almost all the homes in the old part of the village were made of railroad ties. As the mill felled trees and shaped logs for the railroad, they frequently stacked long lengths of hewn logs for quick houses. A walking tour brochure distributed by the El Valle Historical Society directs visitors to a few of the log homes, some of which were made from logs standing on end.

Doc Dunham's house, on the New Mexico Register of Historic Places, was built from 1929 to 1932 by a Swedish immigrant named August Holm, dubbed an artist with an ax. The house was entirely built without power tools or nails and was constructed of round spruce logs with compound dovetailed corners. Doc skinned bear in the basement and performed autopsies in the garage.

When the logging industry slowed down, it left two voids: one economical and one physical. The railroad exhausted pine timber in the immediate vicinity seven years after it came to town. Logging companies then began clear cutting in a wider radius, adding spur railroads to haul logs out of the more distant areas. Hundreds of square miles of forest were completely wiped out. Although logging is still active in the area, its era ended by World War II.

Sheep raising in the Chama Valley filled the voids left by logging. Two decades prior to the coming of the railroad, the valley was first settled by shepherds of Spanish ancestry who founded the villages of Los Ojos, La Puente, and Los Brazos (about twelve miles south of Chama). Their sheep had originally been imported from Spain and were touted as the choice or *churros* from the Spanish Merino herds which produced good hand-spinning and weaving wool. When weaving became a dying form, these sheep were updated by bucks from other breeds which met the current needs for meat and heavy-wool production. Edward Sargent, a politician whose house in Chama is on the walking tour, brought in Rambouillet and Columbia bucks from Utah. By the 1920s, *churros*, now called *navajosa*, could only be found on the Navajo reservation.

Sargent, Burns (the bootlegger we met earlier), and a fellow named Miguel Gonzales owned most of the land and most of the fifty thousand head of sheep in the valley. Many people of the valley raised one or more bands (eight hundred to a thousand) of sheep on shares or *partido* from these old dons at thirty cents a head as a range or pasture fee. The landlords in turn shouldered all the expenses and responsibilities. Three men could watch the herd, but fifteen were required during the lambing season that lasted four to six weeks. They were allowed to sell all the wool the sheep produced and keep three-quarters of the lamb crop, which they usually shipped out by train to Eastern or Midwestern markets. Even successful shepherds lived at subsistence levels, making about $18 to $30 minus what they had to make up for losses caused by disease, hard winters, or predators. The money they did earn paid off their credit at the Burns store in Los Ojos.

The winter of 1931-32, combined with the Depression, ended the sheep industry abruptly. It snowed four feet without stopping one day in mid-November, and it stayed on the ground until April. Winter had arrived earlier than expected, and it followed a few mild winters which allowed people to get careless about putting back hay for the stock and bringing the sheep down to the winter pasture. Thousands of sheep and vast numbers of wild ponies were caught in the north country and died. Chama old-timers remember the horses standing on their hind feet to feed in the trees and consequently hanging themselves in the forks of the branches. Others survived by grazing on horse tails.

Despite the hardships, the families were close, and there was usually plenty to eat. Weddings became major events and were conducted in the tradition of old Spain. The following is a northern New Mexico recipe for a wedding pastry called *puchas*. Note that the recipe calls for *tequesquite*, a crude sodium bicarbonate which forms on the edge of mineral springs. Used in place of soda, it made baked goods extra light and fluffy.

Puchas:

30 egg yolks
1 cup sugar
1 cup lard, melted and cooled
2 teaspoons anise seed
1/4 teaspoon alum (dissolved in a little warm water)
1 cup good bourbon whiskey
1 + cups flour (sifted)
2 tablespoons *tequesquite*

Add *tequesquite* to whiskey stirring a few times and allowing to settle. In large mixing bowl, beat yolks for fifteen minutes, add alum and anise. Gradually add sugar and beat in lard. Blend in one cup of flour by hand. Add small portion of strained whiskey to mixture; continue to add more flour and whiskey to make a medium dough that can be shaped into drop cookies. Drop by teaspoon on floured board to shape and bake on ungreased cookie sheet at 350 degrees for fifteen minutes or until dry and light brown.

Many of the houses in Los Ojos, La Puente, and Los Brazos are still occupied and in good preservation. More than half are listed on state and federal historical registers. Between 1880 and 1920, the Hispanic families called on the skilled Scandinavian tie cutters in Chama to make improvements on their existing homes. Pitched roofs, porches, gingerbread trim, and other Victorian touches were added to the original flat-roof adobes. These turn-of-the-century *alteratopms*, with their northern European influence superimposed on the old Spanish or Pueblo Indian styles, are unique to New Mexico.

In the 1980s, Hispanics formed the Ganados del Valle (livestock in the valley) cooperative to bring back the Churro sheep, the only ones with greaseless, deep black wool. The long-fiber wool is softer in texture and appearance than traditional styles used by Native Americans. The cooperative supplies Tierra Wools, an organization of women who weave rugs, blankets, and clothing in the so-called Rio Grande tradition. Ganados also revived the old *partido* system of raising sheep on shares. Tierra Wools is located at Los Ojos on U.S. Route 84/64 south of Chama in the old Burns store.

Another interesting side trip is Tierra Amarilla, twenty-four miles south of Chama. The name means yellow earth, literally the color of the wildflowers that cloak the valley in the summer. The white territorial courthouse was taken over by Reis Lopez Tijerina and his gang in 1967 to protest court decisions in the Tierra Amarilla land grant dispute, first settled by the sixty or so original residents of Los Ojos, Los Brazos, and La Puente. The land grant extends into Colorado and is still not completely settled. (Land grants were originally granted to loyal soldiers or settlers by the Spanish government prior to 1846 and remained a point of contention statewide well into the twentieth century.) It is a known fact that folks buried in the graveyards around here have been known to sway local and state elections.

Chama's train is its one constant through history. For economic reasons, the D&RG,W filed a petition in 1967 to abandon the entire line from Antonito to Durango and Farmington, and the petition was upheld in 1969. In 1970, the legislatures of New Mexico and Colorado purchased the sixty-four miles of track between Chama and Antonito and leased the new tourist-oriented railroad to Kyle Railways for management. Serious plans by residents are underway for a train museum.

The Cumbres and Toltec Scenic Railroad is today Chama's largest employer. Between Memorial Day and mid-October, as many as four hundred and fifty passengers fill a single trip. The route covers some of New Mexico's most awe-inspiring mountain scenery, traveling though the majestic Toltec Gorge of the Los Pinos River and topping off at the 10,015-foot Cumbres Pass before it descends again into Chama. Tickets vary between $32 and $50, depending upon one's preference for a round trip or to return by van or personal transportation. The latter choice is the most expensive. Sundown and moonlight train rides are also available for $39.95 per person. On that ride, passengers disembark at the halfway point in the Cumbres Pass for barbecue, marshmallow roast, and sing-a-long, and return to the Chama depot by 10:30 P.M.

The train is only a seasonal industry. The lumber industry is also making a come-back, but it is slow and more methodical. The peaks, rivers, lakes, and national forests near Chama also attract tourists interested in hunting, fishing, snowmobiling, and cross-country skiing. Including the accommodations already mentioned, the chamber of commerce lists eighteen motels and lodges. The Oso Ranch and Lodge on the river is owned by Indianapolis 500 winners Al Unser and Al Unser Jr., of Albuquerque. Most of the hotels offer hunting and train packages.

Land developers are still attracted to Chama, but now for the tourism industry. Conflicts have arisen between old-time residents who want to preserve the area and those who want to bring in the engine of progress. Old political factionalism and inaction had much to do with keeping the town from developing a firm growth strategy in the past. Citizens such as Mayor Tony Gonzalez are working to change that. An airport is being built on the Jicarilla Apache reservation near the town of Dulce, thirty miles west of Chama.

Most of the restaurants in town provide box lunches for train passengers. For creative and healthy cuisine, we ate at the Whistle Stop Cafe directly across from the train. I asked a local where she'd eat, after telling her Santa Fe (two hours' drive to the south) didn't count, she immediately suggested Vera's Mexican food, which my sister also recommends. I noticed in the newspaper that reporters can expect a scoop at this local hang-out. My informant also added that Big Vee's has the best green-*chile* (New Mexican natives use the Spanish spelling *chile*, pronounced chee-lay, for the hot pepper) cheeseburger in the state, but I didn't have time to test it.

Winters are still hard in Chama. Alice Nuno said the stranded travelers often end up at Foster's, and in this way, she is able to squeeze through the season. The local paper says you know it's spring when the first train whistle blows; retirees switch from snowmobiles to boats as their primary mode of transportation; everything turns to mud; the rumor mill starts up (no one's exempt); and Alex begins pedalling in shorts through a late snowstorm—whoever Alex is.

For more information:

(Addresses are in Chama, NM 87520)
Cumbres & Toltec Scenic Railroad, Chama Depot, 505-756-2151
Foster's Hotel, 505-756-2296
Chama Station Inn, 505-756-2315
Shamrock Hotel, 800-982-8679
Jones House Bed & Breakfast, 505-756-2908
Oso Ranch & Lodge, 505-756-2954
Whistle Stop Cafe, 505-756-1833
Viva Vera's Mexican Kitchen, 505-756-2557, 756-2374
Chama Valley Chamber of Commerce, 800-477-0149

Additional information:

Tierra Wools, Los Ojos, NM 87551, 505-588-7231

Directions:

In western New Mexico, exit from Interstate 40 at Grants south on New Mexico Route 53. Or exit from Interstate 40 at Gallup south on New Mexico Route 602 to New Mexico Route 53 and head east to Ramah, about halfway between the pueblo/town of Zuñi and El Morro National Monument on New Mexico Route 53. Population: approximately 1,000; elevation: 7,000; county: McKinley.

Highlights:

Early Mormon settlement history; turquoise at the Black Rock Trading Company; Ramah Lake; Ramah Navajo Weavers Association; the well-known Vogt Ranch, now a b and b; El Morro National Monument; the Blue Corn Restaurant and the Stagecoach Cafe.

CHAPTER 3

RAMAH

Hidden Ramah

amah is a "quiet village encircled by alfalfa fields of Irish green," wrote anthropologist Clyde Kluckhohn in his 1933 book, *Beyond the Rainbow.* "Grave Lombardy poplars and irrigation streams flowing on either side of the streets stamp it as Mormon settlement." In his day, lithe Navajos and squat Zuñis wrapped in Pendleton shawls tarried around the Ramah Trading Post, built in 1903 by the English-born Masters brothers. It is the one historic building visible from the highway and it is long abandoned, giving the false impression that Ramah itself is on the decline. This is not the case.

Brigham Young Jr. gave the town its name. In the *Book of Mormon,* precious records were hidden in a hill called Ramah, and in Old Testament Hebrew, Ramah means "high, exalted place." Indeed, the pastoral valleys blend so beautifully with the red mesas around Ramah, you might be mesmerized into driving right through town. Unless your stomach growls about the time you pass the two restaurants or you're tempted to shop for turquoise at the new Black Rock Trading Company, you probably wouldn't think of stopping here. There is more to this shady town than meets the eye, but someone has to tell you where to look.

My decision to explore Ramah was based on a friend's recommendation. Years ago, she had answered an ad offering to fly potential buyers to property in the Ramah area. (Half the people living in New Mexico were brought here under similar serendipitous circumstances.) She provided the key to Ramah's hidden records in a single phone number—the Vogt Bed and Breakfast on the Davis Ranch.

For many decades, the Vogts have played host to anthropologists, archaeologists, western authors, such European dignitaries as the aid to Otto, the Archduke of Austria, and even Barbara Bush (President Bush's sister). Everyone who came knew that Evon Zartman "Easy" Vogt would direct them to hidden treasures in the area, as his grand-daughter, Anita Davis, directed me to the roots of Ramah. She did correctly, for the story does not begin with the town's most illustrious character, but with the Mormons who built the community. We'll return to the Vogt house after first meeting Ramah's earlier residents.

Five rock buildings stand as tribute to the missionaries who built Ramah. I had the pleasure of poking through the Ashcroft and Bond houses and meeting two charming pioneer descendants, Paul Merrill and Jerry Tietjen. Merrill's family bought the Ashcroft house in 1912 after being run out of Mexico by Pancho Villa. Tietjen's family was the first to settle in the area to convert Navajos to Mormonism as early as 1876.

One needs a genealogy chart to navigate through the Mormon family orchards, and although I was in the hands of experts, I quickly lost count of all the wives and children of their great-grandfathers. (Fortunately, these men had a sense of humor.) Both gentlemen are in the process of restoring the Maggie Bond house as a historical mu-seum to help outsiders like myself in following along.

Brigham Young was a Johnny Peopleseed. He directed the coloni-zation of a hundred thousand into three hundred and fifty settlements. In the last year of his life, 1876, he sent missionary families to settle northern Arizona, Mexico, and a few to the Ramah area. Many of these families had been driven from the Midwest by people who dis-approved of their religion. When the Mormons decided to build a town, they did it right. Unlike the random settlement patterns in most of the West, the Mormon colonies were well-planned. A leader was selected in advance and a blacksmith, wagon maker, rock cutter, surveyor, and midwife set up clinics to teach their trades. Each family was issued provisions and an ax.

Despite best-laid plans, the Tietjens and other missionaries to first settle on the Little Cebolla (Spanish for wild onion) Creek five miles to the north of what is now Ramah had a rough time of it. Tietjens

and Burnhams settled a town called Savoia and were later joined by a
half dozen more families including Bonds, Bloomfields, and Ashcrofts.
Ira Hatch also settled in the area at San Lorenzo, also called Old
Tinaja. (See Aztec chapter.) About the same time, two other missionaries, inspired by a vision, came here briefly instead of going to
Mexico and claimed a hundred and sixty-seven souls from the ancient pueblo of Zuñi for the Church. (See Zuñi chapter.)
    A hundred more Mormon converts arrived from Arkansas the fol-
lowing year. Lack of provisions and slim crops forced the newcomers
on to Arizona, but not before they left a wake of smallpox. Disease
and hunger quickly diminished the budding town until all who remained were the Tietjens. They eventually moved into Ramah.
    Samuel E. Lewis along with several other families moved in from
Arizona in 1882 and set up a complete church organization. Originally, the new town was to be called Navajo, but upon applying for a
post office in 1883, they discovered the name redundant, and took
the younger Young's suggestion of Ramah. They outlined the present
town square and built new houses and a large multipurpose building
for meeting, schooling, and dancing—the Mormons love to dance.
They also built a house for the Navajos whom they called the
Lamanites. With new enthusiasm and fresh strength of numbers, they
picked up the old dam project and finished it in three months, thus
creating Ramah Lake. They continued working on the dam over the
next few decades and later dug irrigation ditches and brought water
to Ramah. "Mormons are the only ones who can make water go up-
hill," Merrill said. "It had less than a foot of fall." Merrill worked on
the dam himself at age thirteen.
    Ramah Lake is a favorite fishing spot. There's a sign at the south
end of the lake that says, "Tietjen's Campground, $5 a night; no camp-
ing on this side of fence; keep down the noise; no drunkenness; we've
experienced theft."
    Of the Navajos native to what they call Tl'ochini (place of the wild
onions), only seven or eight families returned to it after being released in 1868 from the enforced reservation at Bosque Redondo,
and most of the population is descended from them. (See Fort Sumner

chapter.) They had lived in the area at least since the sixteenth century. Their first settlement apparently sits at the bottom of the lake created by the Mormon settlers.

Current Navajo literature claims they built the dam, and they mourn the loss of prime land to the early homesteaders. Following the Dawes Act of 1887, most of the Navajo families were allotted 160-acre plots of land left in the public domain; but in 1882, the government had given the Atlantic and Pacific Railroad alternate sections of a strip of land eighty miles wide for the purpose of putting through a line to California. What was left over was kept by the government and given to the Indians, which consisted mostly of unuseable lava rock country called *malpais*. The Navajos live on checkerboard parcels gained in exchange for land with federal, state, and private holders. Additional property was also purchased with funds provided through public law.

The Ramah Navajos are today the largest of several groups of Navajos who live off the main reservation that straddles the New Mexico-Arizona border, governing themselves while keeping cultural and social ties with the main group. The Ramah Navajo Weavers Association, a grassroots cooperative group of more than forty weavers, offers traditional handspun, handwoven rugs and blankets.

Despite what the literature says, there is a sense of a cultural symbiosis. Navajos probably did work on the Mormon dam project and were constantly hired to work on the ranches. The Zuñi, well versed in ancient masonry, were often called in to lay up the corners of the rock houses or help with plastering. Some of the Mormons ran trading posts (including Paul Merrill at Fort Wingate and the Tietjens) which promoted Navajo silversmithing and weaving. Although the traders may have charged high prices, some went broke hauling their goods the long distance to the railroad or from not being able to collect on unpaid bills. The Mormons often tended Navajos when they were sick, and in the winter of 1896-97, when the settlers came down with scarlet fever or small pox, the Navajos left fresh deer meat on the outskirts of town for them.

It wasn't easy for the Ramah Mormons either. Grasshoppers ate the crops in 1888-90, and the sawmill they moved to the Zuñi Mountains from Arizona burned down. In 1889, the Cebolla Cattle Company purchased the townsite and gave notice to the Mormons to leave. The Mormons had intended to buy Section 35 for about fifty cents an acre, but with drought, pestilence, and famine always upon them, they neglected to acquire title. At the price of ten dollars an acre, the Church loaned the village $6,400 to pay the cattle company. Despite the hardships, the Mormons elected to stay in Ramah even after the Church released them.

When Mormons came under fire in 1883 for their practice of polygamy, some escaped to Mexico and built half a dozen prosperous ranching, logging, and fruit-tree colonies. The Bloomfields moved to Casa Grande, then to Colonia Juarez, and Oaxaca, Sonora, and returned to Ramah in 1894. The Ashcroft brothers stayed in Mexico only briefly and returned because Josiah Emer Ashcroft, who became a bishop (there were a number of them in Ramah), wanted to marry a certain young lady, Lafentie Pipkin. In 1891, he built the large rock house on the corner of the streets now called Bloomfield and McNeil. The rocks were hauled from hills around the lake or pulled out of the ancient pueblo ruins, and the mortar was mixed at Timberlake and brought over by wagon.

The Merrills stayed on in Mexico until their colony was surrounded by Pancho Villa's army in 1912, which Paul Merrill says was a thousand men strong. After holding a town meeting, his family left in the middle of the night, fifteen or sixteen of them on a hay wagon. For a year they lived in a covered wagon parked next to the Ashcroft house, which a grandmother, Mame, had already purchased for two wagons, their teams, and a $600 note. Paul Merrill, one of ten children, was born in the house, which was later turned into a hotel.

Rosy and Kenneth Harrington of Albuquerque bought the house in 1983 after visiting the area during frequent fishing trips. On the verge of retirement, they "didn't want to wake up with nothing to do, honey." When Andrew and I visited, Rosy was preparing for the descent of two hundred Ashcrofts upon her home. Every four years they attend a reunion picnic in the Harrington backyard. She swore this was to be her last year, but I have my doubts.

Rosy lived in a RV and worked on the house while Kenneth completed his last six months at his job in Albuquerque. She mixed the cement, plastered, and painted the outside of the house herself. "Oh, it was a mess, honey. There were birds and animals living in here, and you could see the sky right through the roof. Hippies squatted in the house and spray painted the walls black." It took three or four years to make it presentable, and it is now on national and state historical registers.

Like all old houses, this one took on additions. The kitchen still had the original cabinets with built-in sugar bins, a flour bin and grinder, and a pie safe. The Ashcrofts conducted services in the big room for the Zuñi converts on Sunday, and in the next century, it was rented out to telephone workers, teachers, and anthropologists. At one time, it served as an infirmary, but today it is a sitting room. "Everyone in town has slept here at one time or another, honey." A spiral staircase leads to the upstairs loft that slept quite a number of children. Bishop Ashcroft had three wives, not all at once, and something like twenty-seven children. Rosy and I agreed that three women could not have lived in this house at the same time. Outbuildings include a root cellar, a cottage, and an adobe wash house that had separate doors for males and females. A twelve-foot stone-lined well provided water, and gas was made in the carbide pit. Electricity didn't come to Ramah until 1948.

The Joseph Alright Boot Bond home, known as the Maggie Bond house, is also on the National Register and is one block south of the Ashcroft home. Maggie was the daughter of the John Bloomfields, who had lived in Mexico. The style is reminiscent of England, perhaps because of the Bloomfield/Bond English ancestry. Homes in Lancashire, England, were similarly constructed of sandstone, partly because of a law dating back to the 1400s that prohibited wood for threat of fire. The gabled roof with a partial hip resembles a thatched roof.

Completed in 1905, the original home had three large, high-ceiling rooms, but a fourth room was added on the northeast corner where

Ramah Trading Post

the snow tended to pile up. One of the two fireplaces was decorated with a mantel made from a wooden bedstead. The ceilings were covered with painted cheesecloth glued in place with flour. The porch on the front was torn off in 1986 for the dedication of the new Latter Day Saints Church next door. One could enter through either of two doors in the front or one in the back. Black locust trees surround the home, first introduced to provide a tough wood for oxen yokes.

When I visited, the walls had already been replastered and Jerry Tietjen had numbered and dismantled the stones in the newest room and had reassembled them with new mortar. The crew included knowledgeable Zuñi and Navajo workers. Jo Ann Davis, daughter of E.Z. Vogt and member of the museum's board, was disappointed she had not been asked to plaster. "I should have been a Zuñi; I love to plaster and I can make the walls so smooth."

I visited with Jo Ann Davis in her kitchen on the old Vogt ranch. Hummingbirds, sparrows, and squirrels feeding at the horse trough beyond the picture window and the bunnies hopping between sage and piñon distracted my attention. Aunt Betty was also there. Betty Vogt Njos had served as a courier on the Santa Fe Railroad. She'd get on at Winslow, Arizona, and narrate the landscape for the passengers as it passed by the windows, take them on a tour of Isleta Pueblo, and then get them on a bus to catch up with the train in Albuquerque. Douglas Fairbanks was one of her more notable passengers. As part of her uniform, Betty wore a squash-blossom necklace, cowboy hat and boots, and a denim skirt which she claims to have invented by cutting open a pair of jeans and sewing them back together into a long skirt.

True to character, Jo Ann was in the middle of supervising the final stages of a *casita* behind her house. The years and years of plastering the nearby Vogt house trained her for her avocation. She was born second to the youngest of five in her father's house, delivered by a school teacher claiming to be a doctor—a fact that was never verified, not that it really mattered. A closet door now serving as a privacy door for the toilet was shoved under the mattress during the delivery.

Growing up on the Vogt ranch was a lot of work, but after the cows were milked and the logs were split, the Vogt children found amusement in the natural environment. Jo Ann's plastering training came early. They would make little adobe houses up in the rocks and "smooth" out the dirt for roads. The long walk to town for school was made tolerable by pretending that the "smooth" graded road was a cement sidewalk in New York and that she was a secretary on her way to work. They would also make sugared orange rinds and hide them in a coffee can in the woods and return on a hot day for a respite.

The Mormon dances were a much anticipated source of entertainment, and Kluckhohn said a dance in Ramah was not an event because they've been dancing, and dancing well, since childhood. He had decided to give himself a farewell dance, and for nine dollars, he hired a bewhiskered cow-puncher pianist, a fiddler who did a buck-and-wing during intermissions, a sheepherder guitarist, and a "mere callow sprout" mandolin player. "The music is stringy and whiny, but the aboriginal thump is there, and our feet hit the pine floor with gusto" beneath two hanging kerosene lamps. They'd play a two-step, a one-step, a schottische or *varsovienne*, even a Charleston. The men lined up on one side of the room and the women on the other, and "every girl is religiously escorted back to her seat after every dance...and left there." Anita Davis, Jo Ann's daughter, said the ladies would put the children down on quilts to sleep, "but we never slept, and we grew up watching our parents' legs going by." Dances today are performed by a fiddle-and-piano duo, Kirk and Flora Clawson, the local saddlemakers.

At Vogt's insistence, the children supplemented their education with reading and by learning from the many visitors drawn to his personality and knowledge of the area. Kluckhohn, Shirley Vogt's first cousin once removed by adoption, was sent to the Vogt ranch from Iowa in 1922 to rest from a bout of rheumatic fever; a few years later, he returned from Princeton when threatened with tuberculosis. He roamed the countryside on horseback to get fit and in so doing, he cultivated an interest in the prehistoric and present Indian population. The Ramah Navajos provided a rich source for his book, *Navajo Witchcraft*, and he built his career on the Indian communities in the vicinity and the numerous archaeological sites on the ranch. Evon Vogt Jr. also became a noted anthropologist and author.

E. Z. Vogt entered the Ramah picture at the beginning of World War I. A tubercular victim himself, he had first come to New Mexico from Chicago around 1906 and healed himself by living in a tent on an orchard farm in Albuquerque and, later, by working ranches. He also worked in the store and post office on the Pigeon Ranch, which had been the site of the Battle of Glorietta in 1862. (See Pecos chapter.) After a brief sojourn through Europe, brought to an end by the war, he bought land near Ramah and went into the livestock business. In 1915, at age 35, he married his sister-in-law's daughter, Shirley Bergman, fifteen years his junior. After a honeymoon horseback pack trip on the Upper Pecos River east of Santa Fe, they settled in a one-room homestead near Ramah.

Vogt was not a particularly successful rancher. The bank took over his property in 1920, and although he eventually bought it back in 1929 and went into the sheep-raising business with a Texas partner the following year, the harsh winters of the 1930s and the depressed prices of wool devastated whatever financial footing he had found. During the Winter of the Big Snow of 1931-32 (see Chama chapter) he rotated among his nine herds fifty miles from the ranch, even sleeping with them, in an effort to keep them alive. He dragged a pine log hitched to four horses through the snow to create a trail to the lower elevations of Arizona, laced it with bails of alfalfa to encourage the sheep to move along. In this way, he managed to save a fourth of the herd, but the rams failed to breed out of exhaustion.

At the end of World War II, Jo Ann's husband, Paul Davis, revitalized the ranch. He went into partnership with a friend, and with twenty-six shareholders and money borrowed from the Mormon Church, he organized the Ramah Land and Cattle Company. The thirty-three-square-mile ranch helped sustain Ramah's economy to the present day.

Fortunately, ranching was not Vogt's only job. Although his health had prevented him from receiving a college degree, he was a student of history, ethnology, and spoke four European languages, as well as Navajo and Zuñi. This self-imposed regimen served him well when he edited the *Gallup Gazette* and *Gallup Independent* and worked as an agent with the US Indian Service to the Ramah Navajos. He is most noted for his tenure as superintendent of the El Morro National Monument (1917-36), which at first paid him all of three dollars a month.

Sheltering a large natural basin of collected water, the top of El Morro rock was an ideal home for the Anasazi in prehistoric times. Over the millennia, every traveler who camped near the pond, including Spanish Conquistadors and American Army personnel, inscribed their names in the rock. Park Service literature estimates that there are about two thousand separate pieces of graffiti, many of them in exquisite calligraphy. The earliest dated inscription was by Don Juan de Oñate in 1605. Don Diego de Vargas, during his 1692 reconquest of New Mexico after the Pueblo Revolt of 1680, found it necessary to declare in writing that he had conquered for Holy Faith and for the Royal Crown all of New Mexico—at his own expense.

Charles F. Lummis, a prolific historical Southwestern writer, brings the inscriptions into perspective in the following entry in the monument's register on September 1, 1926:

"No other cliff on earth records a tithe with as much of romance, adventure, heroism. Certainly all the other rocks in America do not, all together, hold so much of American history. Oñate here carved his entry with his dagger two years before an English-speaking person had built a hut anywhere in the New World, and fifteen years before Plymouth Rock."

Vogt created an advertising campaign to draw visitors to the rock. He darkened the inscriptions with lead pencil and, in some cases, deepened them to make them more legible. He was given authority to arrest modern graffiti vandals, and two violators were sentenced to hiring a stone cutter to remove their names. Other unwanted names were carefully rubbed out with sandpaper. Despite all of his conscientiousness, some nineteenth-century names, including that of Kit Carson, were accidentally removed in Vogt's absence. Although the National Park Service sprang to his defense, Vogt acknowledged the accident. The masthead on the *Gallup Gazette* he edited states, "No apologies for telling the truth." I guess he meant it.

Credit Vogt for the discovery of the nearby Perpetual Ice Caves, for improving the highway from Gallup to El Morro (through Ramah), and for helping to organize the Inter-Tribal Indian Ceremonial in 1921. The first rodeo was held on his property. The tribes still gather at the Red Rock State Park in Gallup every August to demonstrate their arts and crafts, perform dances, and compete in a rodeo. My father often took us to this event, and my most vivid memory is a line of pickup trucks around the rim of the cliff overlooking the park where the powwow took place.

A main attraction at all fairs and festivals in New Mexico is the Navajo "fry bread" booth. This recipe was published by the Ramah Navajo High School in *Tsa'aszi* (magazine):

Fry Bread:
6 cups unsifted flour
2 tablespoons baking powder
1 tablespoon salt
½ cup instant nonfat dry milk
2 ½ cups warm water
Lard or shortening for frying.

Mix dry ingredients; add water and mix with spoon until you have a soft dough. Knead dough until you get a fine-textured dough. Build a fire. Put thick skillet over open fire and add enough lard to float the dough (about an inch deep). Heat until bubbling. Pinch off a piece of dough (about two inches in diameter). With hands flatten and stretch dough until it is about six inches in diameter and thin. Place flattened dough in hot grease and fry until yellowish-brown on each side. Remove from skillet and stack in dish. Fair attenders sprinkle with powdered sugar and cinnamon, dribble with honey, or top with chili salsa. Serves eight to ten.

Anita Davis runs the only formal lodging on New Mexico Route 53 other than the camping and RV facilities at El Morro National Monument ten miles to the east. Her grandmother, Shirley Vogt, had previously run the place as a guest ranch for a period. Rates were $60 per week per person, including everything but horses, which were $3 a day. When she died just a few years ago, her daughter, Jo Ann, planned to tear the house down until she came up with the idea for the bed and breakfast. The house is very much as Shirley left it, thanks to Jo Ann's constant plastering. Guests can lounge in the main room amongst the brightly colored antique Navajo rugs. It is particularly pleasant to sit on the steps made from rocks pulled from the Anasazi dwellings near the house and contemplate the burgundy hollyhocks along the coyote fence. One can almost feel every nerve in the body slow down to a full stop. Breakfast is served in the big kitchen where Kluckhohn wrote the following paragraphs describing the ranch much as it remains:

"...Into Evon Vogt's Ford truck we pile. We sit on spare tires, gasoline drums, suitcases, and small Vogts. Forty miles to the ranch... bump, bump along. Mesas of orange and black, mesas of shining white rock. The Zuñi Mountains in the distance. Faint and subtle comes the first whiff of sage. Prairie dogs scurry away. A light rain baptizes thin city clothes.

"At last the gracious Ramah hills, the sweet green of Ramah Valley, and then the ranch: a little irrigation stream, a corral of tree branches stuck into the ground, a friendly, rambling rock house set on the last slope of a mesa, overlooking a wide valley. Here, with Evon as our Nestor, we shall buy horses and assemble a pack outfit, meanwhile riding and climbing to harden Eastern muscles. We are content to be here. Gone is the drone of street cars, and only occasionally do we hear the sputter of automobiles. The air is clean and alive with the breath of growing things."

Everyone raves about the gourmet cuisine at the Blue Corn Restaurant, which features blue-corn crab enchiladas in cilantro cream sauce. Alas, it is only open Wednesday through Sunday, and we were there on a Monday. The Stagecoach Cafe, open seven days a week, serves an excellent bowl of chili, as I mentioned to the owner, Mary Panek. "Not bad for a Polack," she said of her husband, Leonard. Apparently, he had suffered a number of coronaries before retiring into the restaurant business and has suffered none since. They specialize in naturally aged steaks, filet minon, and frog legs.

For more information:

(Addresses are in Ramah, NM 87321)
Vogt Ranch Bed and Breakfast, 505-783-4362
El Morro National Monument, 505-783-4226
Black Rock Trading Company, 505-783-4500
Blue Corn Restaurant, 505-783-4671
Stagecoach Cafe, 505-783-4288

Additional information:

Ramah Navajo Weavers, 505-775-3253
Inter-Tribal Indian Ceremonial, Gallup, NM 87301, 800-233-4528

Directions:

Take New Mexico Route 32 south from Gallup and after thirty-two miles, turn right onto New Mexico Route 53 and head west another eleven miles to Zuñi. Population: less than 8,000; elevation: 6,400; on the Zuñi Reservation.

Highlights:

Zuñi, New Mexico's largest and most orthodox pueblo; nearby village of the Great Kivas; Our Lady of Guadalupe Church; the restored St. Anthony's Mission; traditional pueblo dances; A:shiwi A:wan Museum and Heritage Center: Zuñi Craftsmen Cooperative Association; Pueblo of Zuñi Arts and Crafts; Seventh City of Gold restaurant.

CHAPTER 4

ZUÑI
Zuñi at the Center Place

he Zuñi believe they literally live at the center of space and time. The middle of time is the winter solstice which intersects with their village in the middle of the universe. Their tradition tells of their emergence into this, the fourth world from the underworld near the Grand Canyon, and of their travels to the east in search of the Center Place where their Maker instructed them to live. They built several villages during the so-called migrations before finally settling at the middle place, or Itiwanna, in the present village of Zuñi, also called Halona:wa. The middle of the universe was determined by stretching the legs of the water strider equidistant to the four oceans. A large boulder marks the spot.

The archaeological record shows that the El Morro and Zuñi Valleys were sparsely inhabited between 8,000 and 5,000 B.C. Around A.D. 300–400, the hunter-gatherer society shifted to that of farming, and the major crop was corn imported from Mexico. They lived in pit houses that were dug into the earth and covered with a roof of mud and brush suspended on poles. Squash and beans were added to the diet in larger yields, and the pithouses doubled as storage facilities. Around A.D. 1000, the villages along the Zuñi River began to resemble the Anasazi villages at Chaco Canyon. (See Aztec chapter.) The Village of the Great Kivas near Nutria Lakes northwest of Zuñi is a prime example of a Chaco contemporary. This village was occupied until the Chaco system collapsed in the twelfth century, and the population of other Anasazi villages in the El Morro and Zuñi drastically diminished.

Years ago, I visited the Village of the Great Kivas ruins on a museum tour guided by Zuñi artist Alex Seowtewa. The ruins consist of a cluster of three ancient pueblos built into the side of a butte, the largest of which contained two large circular underground chambers or *kivas*. As with many Anasazi great houses, it is a ruin with a view of the valley. The sandstone cliff is a canvas for many pictographs, which Seowtewa told us were sacred messages from the ancestors in the under-world. Since all time is simultaneous, one could consider the messages to apply to the present. Zuñis have since returned to paint hidden cliffs with more recent renditions of the spirit people.

The population ebbed and flowed with the precipitation patterns in the valley, and smaller villages combined into large apartment complexes. By the time the Spaniards first came to Zuñi in 1539, there were six villages: Hawikku, Kechiba:wa, Kyaki:ma, Mats'a:kya, Kwa'kina, and Halona:wa, the present Zuñi village. One of the fables the Spaniards pursued was the Seven Cities of Gold to be found on an island in the Atlantic. These tales were given credibility by the great riches found in the Aztec and Inca empires in Mexico and South America, and they became intertwined with the stories the Indians told of the New World. As a defense strategy, the Indians often told incoming Spaniards that gold could be found at villages on the next horizon.

These tales attracted Fray Marcos de Niza and a black Moorish slave, Estevan, to the Zuñi region in their wanderings from Mexico City. In 1539, Fray Marcos sent Estevan ahead to scout the trail with the instructions that he was to send back a small, medium, or large cross as a gauge to the amount of riches he found. When a messenger returned with a man-sized cross, Fray Marcos knew he had struck gold. Estevan, in the meantime, was killed at Hawikku for his aggressiveness toward the native possessions and women. A few of Estevan's men escaped and caught up with Fray Marcos, who planted a cross within sight of the village, claiming the area for Spain.

Fray Marcos returned to Mexico City and reported that he had found the Seven Golden Cities of Cíbola (buffalo). The governor appointed Francisco Coronado to lead an expedition to the golden cities. His army of two thousand left New Spain in 1540 and headed for Arizona. Coronado lead a smaller contingency to Hawikku, but the Zuñis were waiting for him. During the battle, Coronado's gaudy armor attracted the most arrows and rocks. He was knocked to the ground by three well-placed rocks to the head and an arrow pierced through his foot. Coronado nevertheless won the battle, but rather than finding gold and silver, he found corn and food for his men. Spurred by the promise of riches elsewhere, he explored the area west to the Little Colorado River and as far east as Kansas before returning to Mexico City in 1542.

In 1598, Juan de Oñate received permission to colonize New Mexico and came through Zuñi twice, duly recording his name at El Morro in 1605. (See Ramah chapter.) In 1629, a group of Franciscan friars set up the first missions for converts at Hawikku and Halona:wa. The missionaries met strong resistance from the Zuñis, especially when their own religious beliefs were oppressed. In 1632, the Zuñis killed a missionary and the Franciscans abandoned their pulpits until the 1640s. Spanish rule during the next decades was harsh, and their enforced tribute in crops and resources steep. The Zuñis participated in the Pueblo Revolt of 1680 and burned the churches, sparing one of the priests, some books, bells, an altar, and other religious articles. When Don Diego de Vargas came to Zuñi in 1692 during the reconquest, he saw the altar set up at the hide-out village of *Dowa Yalanne* with candles still burning. De Vargas received the peaceful submission of the Zuñis, who insisted on keeping the Christian items.

Alex Seowtewa said the Zuñis were traditionally a hospitable people and probably didn't really want to participate in the Pueblo Revolt. Zuñi oral history claims that pots of silver and gold were buried under the cornerstones of the mission, and the seeds of different crops and different colors of corn and beans were buried at the center. The church was precious to them, especially considering the Zuñis had gone through much sacrifice in helping to build the church as slave labor.

The Zuñis returned to Halona:wa, the present village, but because of their isolation experienced little contact with the Spaniards throughout the 1700s and early 1800s. As a result they were able to maintain many of their traditional values and practices. The language of Zuñi is not spoken by any other Pueblo tribe.

Today, Zuñi is New Mexico's largest and most orthodox pueblo, yet it looks like many New Mexico towns. Zuñi's business districts incorporate what looks to be a disproportionate number of trading posts, three grocery stores, two of which have gas stations, five restaurants, and a bank. The more modern homes are modest cinderblock or adobe. Not readily apparent is the tendency of the Zuñi to build their loose aggregation of houses along solstice lines radiating from the center of the pueblo. That is, their doorways and windows are oriented toward the places where the sun sets and rises on the winter and summer solstices. Not only does the grid reflect the need to be physically in harmony with an aspect of the cosmos, it may have been born out of an egalitarian attitude toward having certain information available to the whole. The sun priest officiated over the ritual and planting calendar by watching the sun's shadows as it crossed his solstice shrine, thereby enabling him to announce the commencement of certain dances, for instance, but the people liked to mark the sun's travels through their own windows.

When Andrew and I drove through the twisting side streets, we saw women baking in the famed Zuñi ovens, or *hebo':we*, the large adobe beehives between the homes. The ovens, thought to have been introduced to the pueblos by Spanish colonists, are usually built in groups of three. Women construct the ovens from rock, mud, and ashes, and the size is determined by the amount of baking the family does. Once shaped, they are plastered with straw and mud to avoid cracking. A handful of cornmeal thrown into the oven determines whether it is too hot; if it turns dark, juniper brush soaked in water will cool it down enough to turn the corn golden brown. The bread takes twenty to thirty minutes to bake.

The core of the village is virtually invisible to cars passing below on New Mexico Route 53. You will never find the multistoried pueblo as it looked in a late 1800s photograph; it has been replaced by one-story rows of adobe homes clustered around the old mission. Our Lady of Guadalupe Church is just off the main thoroughfare, but you can't drive there directly unless you park and climb a set of stairs hidden in a break in the wall or are adventurous enough to wind through a minimaze of narrow streets. If a visitor avoids being distracted by the other-worldly sights, he or she might be able to follow the signs anyway. But driving there any other time than during business hours is like driving into someone's backyard. You will be greeted with stares. The Zuñis probably have the most complex of all religions in the Southwest, and every aspect of Zuñi life is completely integrated with their religion. Numerous religious organizations, through an intricate system of interlocking ceremonials, interrelate the whole of Zuñi culture. Six esoteric cults, in addition to the ancestor cult to which all Zuñi belong, form the basis of the ceremonialism. Each cult has its own priests, fetishes, rituals, and ceremonial calendar.

The church stands at the physical and figurative center of the village and the Zuñis's theocratic government headed by six directional high priests who serve a practical purpose as well as perform secret religious functions. In the late 1800s, the Zuñis repaired the mission and began using it for their own purposes. Alex Seowtewa's maternal grandfather, for instance, held the position of the High Priest to the North, or *Ka:kwe'mosi'*, meaning House Owner. He was in charge of announcing when it was time to replaster the adobe or fix the roof of the church. Villagers were aligned with one of the high priests or another and were assigned to a section of the church that they were to maintain, as well as an allotment in the cemetery outlined by flagstone.

The Franciscans returned to Zuñi in 1921 and built St. Anthony's Mission and School in the northwest section of Zuñi. After a century of neglect, the old mission deteriorated and was rebuilt between 1966 and 1972. The restoration uncovered many older features of the church and the remains of Zuñis who had been buried beneath its dirt floor. Mass is celebrated in the old church on special days, including the feast day of the patron Saint Anthony.

The walls of the old mission had been painted with murals between 1775 and 1789. Inspired by the restoration, Seowtewa's father, Charlie, or *Machoole* in Zuñi, recalled talk of the faded figures. Inspired, Seowtewa consulted with Old Man Mahooty and Old Man Lonkeena, who were both more than a hundred years old, with blind Old Man Dalahaptewa, Old Man Malanie, and Uncle Oscar Nastacio. All of these men remembered seeing the murals and were able to fill Seowtewa in on the details of the Zuñi disciplinary figures painted on the church walls.

With the blessing of the priests, Seowtewa devised a plan for re-creating the Zuñi religious cycle and painted twenty-four spirit figures called *koko* on the upper half of the high, eight-foot-thick walls. These figures are popularly known as *kachinas*, and many of them are represented by the brightly colored, befeathered wooden carvings sold in the trading posts in Zuñi and all over the Southwest. Seowtewa began on the north wall with the near-life-sized beings associated with the winter solstice, considered to be the beginning of the year. He continued along the points of the compass with seasonal scenes, beings, and local landscape including the mythologically significant red buttes and mountains. Lining the walls below the murals are the traditional Stations of the Cross paintings by various artists, depicting the harmony that now exists between the two religious systems—a generous gesture considering the Catholic failure to convert the Zuñis.

"I'm the kind of person when I put out my interpretation of any colors, I would like to have a meaning expressed, some thoughts behind the painting," Seowtewa said. "Now, we live under two worlds . . . I feel our young people should be able to know throughout their lives, their self-image, their cultural traditions and customary lifestyle." Since he is not "an everyday artist," the murals are a work-in-progress, which he produces with the assistance of his two sons. He spends much of his spare time working with young people.

Famous visitors to the kachina gallery have been Marlon Brando, Waylon Jennings, Ben Kingsley, Harry Belafonte, and Jaqueline Kennedy Onassis. Seowtewa had read that she was one of the top well-dressed women in the world, so as a joke he wore his most worn jeans and was surprised that she, too, had donned denim when she visited. He presented her with a sketch of Jesus gazing over the Zuñi village.

The Old Mission is open Monday through Friday from 10:00 A.M. to noon, and 1:00 P.M. to 4:30 P.M. Visitors must go to St. Anthony's rectory at the east end of town for a guide. It is worth the trouble. The artistic juxtaposition of saints and *kachinas* is, well, awe-inspiring.

Traditional pueblo dances held at the mission are not advertised.

Disrespectful visitors in the past have caused the tribe to close the dances to the public.

One of the most famous dances is the Shalako depicted in Seowtewa's work. This is a winter ceremony, performed in late November or early December. It is a re-enactment of the emergence and migration myths and is also a prayer for rain, health and well-being, and propagation of plants and animals. During the Shalako, the spirits of the dead return to be honored and fed. Songs, prayers, rituals, and costumed representatives of the spirit world are complex and private.

The main event is the nocturnal arrival of the Shalakos at the end of a forty-nine-day preparatory period. Six nine-foot-tall creatures with feathered headdresses, clacking beaks, and piñon-bough collars trot toward the village emitting strange whistling sounds. The long stiff robes covered with geometric patterns and icons conceal the humans beneath them. The Shalakos enter the newly built houses packed with visiting Pueblos, Navajos, and a sprinkling of non-Indians. Brilliant shawls, blankets, and pine boughs cover the wall. Age-old rhythms are beat out by squatting drummers and chanters near the altar at one end of the room. There is ritual, dancing, and feasting until dawn.

Some dances at other pueblos are open to the public, but certain etiquette is recommended. Although the sacred rituals are not held in a traditional church, they require equal reverence. Photography, sketching, or otherwise recording the dances are prohibited and, in fact, binoculars, cameras, and recorders will be confiscated. Do not touch or follow the dancers into the houses. Do not block the dancers or watchers or otherwise disturb them with loud talking and such. Do not bring food or drink to the plaza area or use drug and alcohol while on the pueblo. If you are invited into a home for a meal during the dance, be mindful that eating at the table takes place in shifts, and lingering at the table is considered poor manners. Modest dress is appreciated, although denim and turquoise are appropriate.

The A:shiwi A:wan Museum and Heritage Center in Zuñi is a community-oriented museum which provides educational and cultural opportunities to Zuñis of all ages. (The Zuñi call themselves *A:shiwi*. The word Zuñi may be a Spanish approximation of a Tewa or

Keresan Pueblo word *soonyee-ongwee*, meaning "casting place pueblo" or "rock slide pueblo.") Based in exhibit space and offices adjacent to the tribe's Arts and Crafts Enterprise on New Mexico Route 53, the museum is open to the public. Exhibits in the past have included: "Traditional Waffle Garden" displaying native horticulture; "Zuñi through History;" and a photographic exhibit called, "Zuñi and Its People: Now and Then." A book of cartoons by Phil Hughte entitled, *A Zuñi Artist Looks at Frank Hamilton Cushing*, was published by the museum as a humorous commentary on the attitudes of the anthropologists who imposed themselves on the Zuñi near the turn-of-the-century. The museum office is open weekdays from 9:00 A.M. to 4:30 P.M., and the gallery is open Monday through Saturday, 9:00 A.M to 6 P.M. Admission is free, but donations are welcome.

Zuñi jewelers are famous for their turquoise-and-silver petit-point earrings, pendants, and necklaces. Tourists may purchase Zuñi and other Pueblo and Navajo jewelry, pottery, and rugs from a variety of private enterprises as well as the Zuñi Craftsmen Cooperative Association and the tribally owned Pueblo of Zuñi Arts and Crafts.

Zuñi offers five restaurants, one of which is called Seventh City of Gold. Fishing at Ojo Caliente and Nutria Lakes is allowed with a permit obtained at Major Market or the main Tribal Building.

Zuñi is indeed the center of the universe. The town may be thirty-five miles from the railroad and interstate near Gallup, but it was traditionally the crossroads of the trade network between the Rio Grande Pueblos and the Gulf and Valley of Mexico. Its residents need not travel to discover what lies beyond the next mountain range or ocean, and they don't. Yet, the Zuñi arts are known around the world. Cafes in San Francisco, San Antonio, and Paris are named Zuñi, and the Zuñis own stores in San Francisco and Los Angeles. Far more exciting to them is the tight cultural ecosystem in which they live spurred by their busy ritual calendar, values, gossip, and criticism. Their world view is shaped by the details within their small town, reservation, and garden plots. Whatever the Zuñi need is close at hand, and if it isn't, it will soon come to them.

For more information:

(Addresses are in Zuñi, NM 87237)
A:shiwi A:wan Museum and Heritage Center, 505-782-4403
Tribal Offices, 505-782-4481
Arlen Shewka for personal tour of
    Zuñi Pueblo and ruins, 505-782-2560
Pueblo of Zuñi Arts and Crafts, 505-782-5531
Zuñi Craftsmen Cooperative Association,
    505-782-4521 or 505-782-4425
Saturday Tours of Mission, 505-782-4477
Fishing and Hunting Permits on Pueblo, 505-782-5851

Additional information:

Pueblo Cultural Center, Albuquerque, NM 87107, 505-843-7270

Directions:

Exit Interstate 25 at Socorro and find U.S. Route 60 at the southern end of town; head west twenty-seven miles to Magdalena. Population: 1,000; elevation: 6,548; county: Socorro.

Highlights:

The Kelly Mine, visitors' rockhounding, and the town's rich mining past; sheep and cattle ranching; the historic Magdalena Hotel; public campgrounds; the Boxcar Museum; Evett's Cafe and Fountain; the annual Old Timer's Reunion.

CHAPTER 5

MAGDALENA

Trails End in Magdalena

Every July, Navajo, Hispanic, and Anglo families dress up in historic clothing and festively look back on the days when a branch of the Atchison, Topeka & Santa Fe Railroad converged in Magdalena with the hundred-mile-long cattle drive-way from the west and the two-mile spur from the nearby Kelly mines. For a time, Magdalena was one of the largest shipping centers in the Southwest—and also one of the rowdiest. At its peak, the streets bustled with wagonloads of weathered pioneers, fiery ranchers, and grimy-faced miners. Today, Magdalena is just another western drive-through with a shady past.

This is the "trails end," say the billboards and brochures. An ironic motto considering that what is most interesting about Magdalena is no longer visible. Although Magdalena's history begins much earlier, 1884 is celebrated as the year when it became an official town in anticipation of the railroad line opening up from Socorro. The ranching, merchandising, and mining industries took off like a locomotive. All totaled, the train freighted away tons of ore, thousands of head of cattle, thousands of bales of wool, and millions of board feet of timber in exchange for just about anything the producers couldn't produce themselves. Many of the warehouses, mercantile stores, cattle pens, hotels, bars, and gambling dens that had sprung up almost overnight were destroyed by fire or now lie fallow. Except for the Annual Old Timers' Reunion and various fiestas, only a few locals and tourists stroll along the sidewalks or dodge their cars between the semi-trucks, cattle trailers, and recreational vehicles barreling noisily through town. Magdalena is not even a tourist trap, but then, that's part of its charm.

Andrew and I approached Magdalena from the west on U.S. Route 60, the Ocean to Ocean Highway that follows the historic cattle driveway through Socorro County. "Here the Titanic forces of nature, seemingly, have had their playground," writes historian Ralph Emerson Twitchell. ". . . for they reared mountain mass upon mountain mass, not running in parallel ridges but consisting of apparently independent groups and knots thrown up in a haphazard fashion." Topography varies, including salt lakes of great depth, vast stretches of grass-covered plains and fertile valleys, mountain torrents and rivers, large forests, and desolate alkali flats and barren plains.

We drove through the trucking towns of Quemado, Pie Town, and Datil, through the Cibola National Forest where Titanic forces were again active, and through the Very Large Array telescopes spread out surrealistically across the Plains of San Augustin. The otherwise-scenic tour was made miserable by a heat wave, road construction, and one of Andrew's rare migraines. We waited in line for long intervals while the road crews dynamited the earthen shoulders of the old highway, scooped up the pulverized rock, and laid down fresh tar mixed with truckloads of the recycled rubble. When traffic moved, it really moved, kicking up gravel showers against the windshield. (You know you're in trouble when you pass the explosives truck!) We finally reached Magdalena a few hours later than planned, and it truly felt like the end of an excruciatingly long trail.

A root-beer float at Evett's Cafe and Fountain quenches the thirst and soothes the shattered nerves of the weary traveler. This is not a replica of an old fountain, but the genuine article of the sort that rewards explorers of country towns. Named after the former owner of a drugstore in the same location and one-time mayor, Red Evett, the Registered red brick two-story building was once the Magdalena Bank, chartered in 1906. The WPA laid the sidewalk in front in 1938.

With belly up to the counter beneath a continuous stream of cool air blasting from the swamp cooler, we took in the wooden floors, the pressed-tin ceiling, the tinged Nesbitt's Orange Drink posters covering the bubble-gum pink walls. Glass cases display old cash registers, adding machines, radios, and vintage soda-fountain equipment including an aluminum hot-fudge bucket. A sign announces today's pizza and features the Sidetrack Special with bacon, pineapple, and jalapeño and the Magdalena Steer Pie topped by—what else?—hamburger and green chili. Owner David Maitland, of Taos, New Mexico, had recently saved the cafe from permanent closure almost as a public trust for the ranchers and Navajos who make frequent pilgrimages for the green-chili dishes.

Evett's is on the corner of U.S. Route 60 and Main. For all of its current under-use, Main is an overly wide street leading to the tracks and train depot. Across the street from the depot is the handsome brick Charles Ilfeld Co. A "wholesaler of everything," this was one of Magdalena's earliest businesses and one of the last to close. The building now belongs to Eagle Wholesale and is on the State Historic Register. The town newspaper, the *Magdalena Mountain Mail and High Country Round-Up* is housed in another comely red-brick building between Evett's and the depot. Publisher Jacky Barrington is self-appointed caretaker of the town's archives, and the newspaper office is known to take walk-in traffic. It was closed when we were in town.

A sign invites visitors to the Boxcar Museum parked at the dock of the shady yellow depot. It was closed. I inquired at the library inside the old dock warehouse and the librarian stuck her head out the door. "Mr. Burson, do you have the keys to the boxcar?" One of the men clustered in conversation in the parking lot came up the stairs and slid open the door while explaining that the docent, one of the town's more talkative old-timers, was probably home taking a nap.

The box car was like an oven, but this didn't stop Jim Burson from going over the few historical photos, antiques, clothing, and other odds and ends the museum had managed to collect. ("We're still in the organizational phase.") About twenty minutes into his enthusiastic commentary, during which he suggested twice that I register at his motel (Western Motel) for a few days to talk to some of the old people, he mentioned that he was the mayor.

The train depot now serves as town hall; the ticket master's office is occupied by the village clerk. Town meetings take place in what was the passenger's lobby. Some of the graffiti carved into the wooden walls by dockworkers was retained in what is now the library. A smaller version of the present train depot was built in 1907, but after it was destroyed by fire, it was replaced by a 6500-foot Standard Number 4 branch-depot kit in 1917 and was painted yellow in the 1930s or 40s, courtesy Sherwin-Williams paint made with lead from Kelly Mine. Mayor Burson plans to return the color to its original Victorian red.

The mayor was kind enough to give me an overview of the town's past and what better place to start than from the perspective of Magdalena Mountain. For there, outlined in evergreen, is a feminine profile and bust carved in stone by the same Titanic forces. Seeing the image, a small group of Spanish soldiers in the 1540s were re-minded of a similar formation in the Sierra de Magdalena in Spain and thus named the image in honor of the repentant woman from Magdala (Mary Magdalene). The New Mexico town that grew up at her feet took her name with the Spanish pronunciation. According to legend, the image marked a sanctuary for fugitives, and Mary Magdalene appeared in spirit to frighten away Apaches who had sur-rounded a Mexican party. She is also said to have pointed to the bounty of ore buried in the mountains. Miners and cowboys looked to Lady Magdalene in repentance for a lusty life of drinking, brawling, and gambling. Before Magdalena was voted "dry" and bootlegging com-mandeered business from the saloons, the town had more than its share of bars and casinos. There was even a horse track for quarterhorse and thoroughbred racing.

Nomadic Native Americans and a few scattered Spanish and Mexi-can settlements had Magdalena country to themselves until post-Civil War soldiers stationed at the nearby territorial forts began prospect-ing there. In 1866, Colonel J. S. "Old Hutch" Hutchason discovered lead on the western slopes of the Magdalena Mountains, and several camps, including Kelly, were established by miners and merchants within the next five years. (There followed nearly ninety years of lead, zinc, silver, copper, and gold mining.)

Meanwhile, a few ranches began to grow in the crevices. In those days, a ranch was nothing more than a log or rock shack and a small corral next to a spring. A rancher, who survived by being meaner than everyone else, built up his herd by shearing off the "sooners,"

Magdalena

the brandless calves belonging to his neighbors, friend, or foe. If a guest happened to comment on his steak, the rancher often replied, "That's one of yours. Don't you recognize it?"

In 1878, William Raymond Morley surveyed the county on behalf of the Santa Fe Railroad for a route to Yuma, Arizona. He concluded that the rugged countryside suited cattle but would not be conducive to railroad track. His business partners took his advice and moved some of their operations to the region. Morley was manager of the Maxwell Land Grant, the centerpiece of the Colfax County War (see Cimarron chapter) and after his accidental death in Mexico where he was chief engineer in the building of the Mexico Central Railroad, his wife and children settled in the Datil area to raise cattle. His son and namesake became a cattle legend and his daughter, Agnes Morley Cleveland, an author. In her book, *No Life for a Lady*, she said Magdalena, which reached a population of three thousand at its peak (twice what it is now), was the closest they had to civilization.

Civilization is in the eye of the beholder. Agnes's mother, Ada McPhearson Morley, arrived in Magdalena with her children in 1886 and when checking into the hotel, she requested they not be put in a room over the bar where stray bullets could come up through the floor. Mrs. Morley was justified in her concerns, and the rowdiness only got worse in the days when cattle-shipping by rail began to take off and miners and cowboys stalked the streets with whiskey under their belts looking for excitement. Agnes, who later operated a motel on Highway 60, commented on the fact that it was accepted as a matter of course that male guests in a hotel would share their quarters with subsequent arrivals, friend or stranger, even three in a bed. Cowboys and shepherds were constantly brawling while awake, so they made poor bedfellows by night. It has been said that were all the men killed in Magdalena laid end to end, one could walk on dead men from the upper end of the business district all the way to the train depot. A local saddlemaker gave up replacing his bullet-riddled windows, but that wasn't the worst of it. When a man dropped dead right in the middle of their transactions for a new saddle, he turned and ran so fast, men could have played cards on his coat tail.

But when Morley issued his negative rail report in 1878, Magdalena had not even been conceived of yet, although mining in the region continued to poke along. Then, in 1881, Gustave Albert Billing, a German immigrant who had had financial success in Leadville, Colorado, acquired the Kelly Mine for $40,000 and put a force of men to work. Seeing a need for a large smelter, he invested $300,000 in the construction of several more outside of Socorro. E.W. Eaton's Patterson Canyon Smelter near Kelly was the first lead smelter in the Southwest, but it wasn't large enough to handle the considerable needs of the entire district. In an unprecedented display of coordinated activity, the land, water rights, and right of ways were acquired, machinery ordered, and construction on the smelters begun. By January of 1884, three smelters had produced 2,303 tons of base bullion, amounting to one hundred eighty-five railroad carloads of about twelve and a half tons each.

On May 5, 1884, the above-mentioned historian Twitchell, clearly

privy to insider's information as an attorney in the firm representing
the AT&SF Railroad and its subsidiary, the New Mexico Town Company, sold 518.74 acres for a dollar an acre to Richard Wilder who
represented both interests. Three days later, a town-site deed was filed
with the county and Wilder, now the owner of all the land plotted as
the town site, began selling small lots for $35 each. Thus Magdalena
was born, poised to serve the region's proliferating mining, ranching,
and freighting industries.

It was Billing's energy and resources that finally persuaded the railroad to put in the line from Socorro to Magdalena with a mine spur
to within a mile of the Kelly mine. He finally made a personal guar-
antee to the AT&SF that Kelly would provide ore shipments suffi-
cient to justify the investment. Years later, the railroad bragged that
the Magdalena branch was their best-paying thirty miles of road.

Until the silver and lead market crashed in 1893, the Magdalena
district produced $6,000,000 worth of ore. In 1904, the Tri-Bullion
Smelting and Development Company of Chicago bought the Kelly
Mine from the Billing family while Sherwin-Williams Paint Co. purchased other mines in the district. The combined mines shipped out
nearly eight million pounds of zinc that year, breathing new prosperity into the area.

The district produced $50 to $60 million in ore between 1886 and
1945, but had hit its peak before the beginning of the Depression in
1929, although intermittent mining and exploration continued. It is
believed that substantial reserves of zinc and lead sulphide ore are
still present in at least three of the mines, but extensive reclamation
won't start again until the price of zinc warrants it. The zinc carbon-
ate, which turned paint a nice bright white, is from a rare variety of
ore called smithsonite, named for its discoverer, James Smithson,
whose bequest established the Smithsonian Institution. A silhouette
of the head frame, supporting a forty-foot elevator, is still visible at
Kelly. It was designed by Eiffel—yes, of the Paris tower fame—and
made of Carnegie steel. "Kelly is the microcosm of the major players
in the late 1800s," the mayor boasted.

The Kelly mining camp had become a proper town in its own right, and at its height, it was home to three thousand people. Though a ghost town now, some feast days are still held in the Catholic Church, and is considered one of Magdalena's major attractions only a few miles away. The Kelly Mine is open to visitors May to October, Friday to Sunday, from 10:00 A.M. to 4:00 P.M.—upon signing a waiver to assume all responsibility for personal safety. Tickets are available at most of Magdalena's restaurants, gift shops, and motels, as well as at Tony's Rock Shop on the road to Kelly. For $10, a person is permitted to collect ten pounds of azurite, barite, quartz, or smithsonite.

The Graphic-Waldo graphite mine, or the Waldo as it is called by the locals, is within hiking distance of the Kelly. In the past, students of the New Mexico Technical and Mining Institute have been allowed to explore, drill, and muck in portions of the Waldo's forty-two miles of tunnels. Old mines and shafts can be dangerous and should not be entered without permission from the owners. My brother, as a geological engineering student at Tech, does not recall seeking permission when he and my other geologist brother explored the creaking mine shafts of the Waldo, but commented on the availability of rental equipment on campus for just such an exploration. The public can view Magdalena's mining history and specimens on terra firma at the mineral museum, operated by the New Mexico Bureau of Mines, on New Mexico Tech's campus in Socorro.

Mining is only a slice of Magdalena's historical past; sheep and cattle ranching sustained the area's economy for decades. Once again, when the people of Magdalena set out to do something, they did it in a big way.

When Solomon Luna, one of the largest wool producers in the state, brought his first string of wagons loaded with wool to Magdalena's dock in 1897, the entire clip of about six hundred sacks had to be piled on the ground. Two of his men guarded the wool until it could be loaded onto the train and shipped out. The Becker Blackwell Company (which later became the Becker MacTavish Mercantile) saw the need for a larger warehouse and quickly expanded their facilities by the time Luna brought in his next clip, this time numbering nine hundred bags. As the wagons arrived, each sack of wool was weighed, numbered, marked, and insured against fire hazard, and later in the season, buyers from the east were invited to examine the clip and bid on it. When hearing of the warehouse, the Aragon family drove a caravan of thirty to forty wagons from their ranch seventy-five miles west of Magdalena down Main to the facility (hence the unusual width of the street). When the Spanish-American War of 1898 caused a flurry of uneasiness in the wool market, a shipment of more than a thousand bags from a community in Arizona was stored on an open porch along the south side of the warehouse facing the Allen Hotel. It was not moved to market until the following year, and it had remained undisturbed the entire time.

The New Deal and the advent of trucking eventually took the wool market from Magdalena and with it, the trade and money in circulation for handling, storing, and shipping crops. The wool was loaded on trucks and whisked through Magdalena to a wool warehouse in Albuquerque. The wool market declined as synthetic materials glutted the market. Weeds flourished in overgrazed areas, some proving deadly to sheep. The coyote population exploded as the government placed restrictions on poison and hunting as the sheepman's only method of control proved ineffective. Today, Navajos on the Alamo reservation twenty-nine miles north of Magdalena still tend smaller flocks of sheep for mutton and wool, but the big sheep ranches are gone.

Turn-of-the-century Magdalena served as the shipping and buying point for cattle ranches within a two-hundred-mile area north, west, and south of the town. Cattle drives joined up with a traditional trail that led into the town. But just as fencing had finished off the Chisum and Loving-Goodnight trails (see Fort Sumner chapter), ranchers began to fear that access through the variously owned lands between the ranches and the town would be similarly cut off. In 1916, the New Mexico Cattle & Horse Growers Association and the New Mexico Wool Growers Association petitioned the Secretary of Interior for withdrawal of certain lands for a drive-way to move stock from summer and winter ranges to Magdalena. This act was not without its controversy, for settlers felt that the potential expansion of their homesteads would be limited. Conflicts were resolved, and the lands along the original trail were withdrawn. The drive-way varied in width from one quarter to five miles and contained about seventy-one thousand acres.

In 1935, the Civilian Conservation Corps (CCC) enclosed the drive-way between Datil and Magdalena with two hundred miles of 5-wire range fence. Nine wells were developed at ten-mile intervals to insure adequate water for the trail herds. In 1946, the ranchers met again to form an association to manage the drive-way as a response to the Grazing Service budget cut. But by 1960, the trucking industry bypassed the drive-way, now controlled by the Bureau of Land Management which began leasing sections to local ranchers. In 1978, the sale of donated parcels by the last two officers of the association helped build the Good Samaritan Nursing Home at the Magdalena edge of Socorro.

The mayor and I stood at the front window of the former passenger lobby facing Main, and with hand gestures, he showed me where thousands of cattle, driven by the smell of those watering intervals, were herded into stock pens at the end of the drive-way just across the street. I could almost see the clouds of dirt kick up in the summer heat. He pointed out the Becker MacTavish Mercantile and the Aragon Hotel, and I strained to see those, too. "Oh, they're not there anymore," he said. "Fire."

Fire was another factor that kept Magdalena businesses hopping and ultimately contributed to the invisibility of its past. To a town with a water shortage and buildings constructed of and heated by wood, fire was an ever-present threat. The most destructive fires took place in winter or spring when the winds fanned the flames. Firefighting was limited to a horse-drawn cart with a water tank. A large section of residences and businesses burned prior to 1900, and in 1918, the Magdalena Hotel became the first of four hotels to burn down in the town's history. It wasn't until 1920 that the Village Board acquired a fire engine, but a pumper does no good without water, and in 1930, fire gutted the Catholic Church. During the 1920s when the cattle market dropped, the banks closed, mining activity decreased, and businesses failed, insurance fires offered a way out. When the economy picked up again in the 1940s, there were mysteriously fewer fires. Adobe buildings slowly replaced the crisp wooden ones, and eventually brick became the primary building material. The Magdalena Hotel, a grand structure with a wrap-around balcony on the second floor, was rebuilt, and although it closed in 1972, it is under renovation.

John Sinclair MacTavish was usually the first to respond to the fire bell with extinguishers. His own store, the Becker MacTavish Mercantile, went up in 1952 in a blaze so hot, the water hoses started melting and the tires on the fire truck smoked. When it looked as though the truck and possibly the men would be lost, one fireman ordered the hoses cut as he drove the truck away, the steering wheel scorching his hands. MacTavish was more than a firefighter, store clerk, and postmaster. He helped weave the economic textiles of Magdalena. Scottish born, he came to this country in 1887 looking for business opportunities and moved to Magdalena in 1897. He became president of Magdalena's first bank in 1910, and it was largely through his "instrumentality" that the Ocean to Ocean Highway came through Magdalena, allowing trucking to become prominent and ultimately leading to the demise of the train in 1973.

The highway drew a new kind of tourism industry as automobilists were drawn to the wildernesses and national forests in the region. Hunting season became busier than cattle-shipping season for the hotels and cafes, but as the cars became more practical, the smaller motels replaced the large hotels. Now, tourists might stop at Evett's for a green-chile cheeseburger and perhaps a slice of homemade pie— and then drive on.

Ranchers are still important players in Magdalena's economy, and a good portion of them in this part of New Mexico publicly support a return to a life free of environmentalists, gun laws, national forests, and grazing restrictions and fees. Who could blame them? Nevertheless, the U.S. Forest Service, which established its headquarters in Magdalena in 1910, is the town's most continuous employer and still cares for much of the beautiful mountain and ranch land that sustained the early settlers. The national forest areas offer a hundred and twenty miles of trails for recreational use, and the adjacent Mount Withington and Apache Kid Wilderness Areas in the San Mateo

Mountains offer another eighty miles of trails for exploring, hiking, and solitude. Developed campgrounds are available at Water Canyon, Beartrap, Huges, Springtime, Datil, and Luna Park, which are rarely fully occupied even on summer holidays.

During the summer months, a number of celebrations and fiestas take place in the area. By far the largest and best known is the Old Timer's Reunion the weekend after Independence Day in July. Activities include rodeos, parades, dances under the stars, watermelon-eating contests, greased-pig chases, Navajo, Hispanic, and local arts and crafts, and the crowning of the Old Timer's Queen.

Participants of the Old Timer's Reunion come in costume typical of the period-—occasionally one will see a flash from a silver spur, a glimpse of a riding crop, the twitch of a white handlebar mustache, or the gleam of handmade Mexican boots, all earmarks of the rugged individual. Conversations lean toward the shape of the ranching industry today, the weather, health, and the sons and daughters who've gone to bigger cities. As the parade of buckboards creak down the main streets past boarded-up buildings and vacant lots healed to green from old flames, some of the old-timers remember when as children they rode into Magdalena in the same rigs for supplies at Salome Store, which since 1910 never closed its doors through all the fires, gun battles, or fiscal glory and ruin.

For more information:

(Addresses are in Magdalena, NM 87825)
Western Motel (reservations recommended), 505-854-2415
Woman on the Mountain Inn (motel and restaurant), 505-854-2747
Evett's Cafe and Fountain, 505-854-2449
Old Timer's Reunion, 505-854-2261
Rockhounding at Kelly Mine, 505-854-2415
Magdalena Mountain Mail and High Country Round Up, 800-854-2719
    or 505-854-2482
Cibola National Forest District Office, 505-854-2281

Additional information:

Indian Day Celebration at Alamo Navajo Reservation, 505-854-2686
Very Large Array (VLA), radio telescope facility and visitors center,
    505-772-4011

Directions:

Truth or Consequences is 151 miles south of Albuquerque on Interstate 25 and seventy-five miles north of Las Cruces or 118 miles north of El Paso, Texas, on Interstate 25. Population: 6,500-7,000; elevation: 4,260; county: Sierra.

Highlights:

A town named by a radio show; hot springs in the marshes; Geronimo Springs Museum; Callahan's Auto Museum; nearby Elephant Butte Dam and Elephant Butte Lake State Park; Dam Site Restaurant; Blue Note Cafe; Artesian Bath House.

CHAPTER 6

TRUTH OR CONSEQUENCES

*From Geronimo's Spring to Game Show
in Truth or Consequences*

illions of years ago, tumultuous powers cast up the mountains and drained the sea that once covered the middle Rio
Grande valley. As a result, the entire downtown area of
Truth or Consequences sits atop an abundant supply of ther-
mal mineral water that bubbles to the surface in pools and wells. The
springs were once used by prehistoric peoples, and in this century, a
municipality grew up around the mineral-bath business. Construction
of nearby Elephant Butte Dam, resulting in the largest manmade lake
in the state, boosted the town's growth almost from the beginning. Retirees, campers, boaters, and health seekers still come to the waters.

The town itself is not exactly picturesque. The arid, dusty climate
best suits cactus and sunning rattlers, and the gray-to-brown terrain
against the washed-out sky scorches eyes more accustomed to lush
hues of green. But under closer scrutiny, the desert holds a subtle beauty
for those who learn to detect the red fruit of Christmas cactus, the
silvery leaves and indigo petals of sage, or the white, velvet-edged
trumpet blossoms of the (hallucinogenic) thorn-apple plant. The
motels, row apartment houses, cafes, RV dealerships, and gift shops
crowd the main streets along the Rio Grande between the Turtleback
and Mud Mountains seemingly without forethought of design. But
few of the earlier buildings were built in that grand territorial style of
whitewashed adobe with broad wooden beams and wall murals developed by the WPA projects of the 1930s.

Long before the advent of Spanish exploration and American fran-
chise, the native population gathered here (and at other springs in
the region) to bathe in the steamy waters. The hot springs were con-

sidered neutral zones, and warriors were protected from the threat of attack while they soaked their aching muscles and packed their battle wounds with the thick white clay. Legend has it that when the Spaniards finally stumbled upon the springs, a tribal leader told them where to look under a large flat rock hiding the most powerful waters and healing muds. The Spanish term for hot springs is *ojo caliente*, literally meaning hot eye. Northern Pueblo peoples believe the hot springs to be entryways to the underworld where the Creatrix lives.

Despite this romantic view, relations between the natives and the paler newcomers were far from cordial. When, in 1605, the Spanish Crown established the Camino Real (royal road) between Mexico and Santa Fe for explorers and colonizers along the Rio Grande, it passed right through the hot-springs area. To avoid native hostility, however, travelers rerouted through a ninety-mile stretch of desert called Jornada del Muerto (route of the dead man) between the Caballos and the San Andres Mountains. The route was marked by waterless, treeless, grassless campsites spaced a day's journey apart.

In 1688, a German trader fleeing from heresy and witchcraft charges, died along the Jornada presumably at the hands of his Indian servants or Apache raiders. All that could be found were a few bones gnawed on by animals and some scraps of velvet. The campsite was named *El Aleman* (the German) in the dead man's honor and it later became part of the Aleman Ranch. During the Pueblo Revolt of 1680, as many as five hundred and seventy-three Spaniards perished while crossing the Jornada. In 1857, camels were imported by the U.S. Congress to enable California-bound expeditions from Texas to more safely cross the Jornada. Operation Camel was discontinued at the outbreak of the Civil War, and the coming railroad made the idea obsolete. By 1881, the Atchison, Topeka and Santa Fe followed the Camino Real through the Jornada del Muerto.

The floods of water, culture, semantics, and time have made tracing the origin of Truth or Consequences problematic. From Spanish accounts, we know that they established a mission on the Rio Grande at a place called Las Palomas sometime in the seventeenth century, although the exact location is not clear. *Palomas* refers to the thousands of doves that nested in the cottonwoods along this section of the river. The mission became an important trading post on the Camino Real and provided protection and shelter for the pack trains unable to ford the river during flooding seasons, which often lasted weeks at a time. Four Spanish families settled a farming community (presumably near the mission) called Las (originally Rio) Palomas in 1856 (or 1863 or 1865). The community was established at what is today called Palomas Gap, the place where the Palomas Creek empties into the Rio Grande.

The hot springs in the marshes seven miles to the north of Las Palomas naturally became known as Palomas Ojo Caliente. The Anglo town that grew up around the springs a half century later took on its name, but in history and guide books, that town never gained a separate identity of origin from the Spanish community of Las Palomas. The confusion is compounded by the fact that New Mexico has a number of places called Ojo Caliente. Eventually, Palomas Ojo Caliente became simply Hot Springs, and in the 1950s, it was renamed Truth or Consequence and shortened to T or C over the decades.

Fort McRae (1863-1876) was among the minor military establishments in New Mexico protecting the Rio Grande valley. The adobe post was situated near a sweet-water spring in McRae Canyon, which was the last place where one could travel between the Jornada del Muerto and the river without going over a mountain. On the old maps, this location was called Ojo del Muerto, which either refers to a hot springs or the passageway to the Jornada. The fort commanded the Apaches's prized water rest at Palomas Ojo Caliente ten miles to the west, which was supposedly frequented by Geronimo. At one point, while the soldiers were picnicking near the spring, Apaches attacked and stole their wives, horses, and shoes, and they were forced to walk back to the fort barefoot.

To further complicate matters, Fort Ojo Caliente was established in 1859 near Monticello about twenty-two miles northwest of Palomas Ojo Caliente. In 1874, Fort Ojo Caliente served as headquarters for the Southern Apache Agency before the establishment of Ojo Caliente Reservation, also known as Warm Springs Apache Reservation. The name of the reservation, which is now part of the Cibola National Forest, was taken from yet another hot springs located about twelve miles upstream from Monticello. Geronimo liked sitting in these natural baths. However, the 1876 Department of Interior map of the Territory of New Mexico shows both the reservation and the community of Hot Springs on the Rio Grande, which may explain the fusion of legends.

The Apaches of the Alamosa Box actually requested the reservation at Ojo Caliente (near Monticello), which they claimed as their homeland. The hostility of white settlers towards the Apaches, suspected Indian Rings in Washington, and contractors and profiteers instigated a plan to remove the Apaches to San Carlos Reservation in Arizona, described as "Hell's Forty Acres." This action led to Indian uprisings and raids, including the Victorio War, and the Loco and Geronimo campaigns. In 1876, an Indian agent from San Carlos, backed by a group of Apache militia, captured Geronimo and his party of Chiricahua Apaches while they were bathing in the hot springs near Monticello. Geronimo and a number of Apaches escaped from San Carlos the following year and agitated military authorities in southern New Mexico for a number of years. Things didn't settle down in Sierra County until he was captured in Oklahoma in 1886.

Buffalo Soldiers (a troop of black enlisted men) from Fort Ojo Caliente had engaged the Apaches in a bloody battle at the mining town of Chloride. Other mining towns in the hills of the Mimbres Mountains and the Black Range west of Palomas Ojo Caliente (T or C) also carried the brunt of the Apache rage. Gold and silver had been discovered there beginning in 1877, giving impetus to a mining boom that lasted several years.

Hillsboro, a name which was literally drawn from a hat, became the center of the mining district and the Sierra County seat when it was created in 1884. Hillsboro was the venue for the circuslike trial concerning the murder of Colonel Albert Jennings Fountain (see Mesilla chapter) and also the home of one Sadie Orchard. Born in London as Sara Jane Creech, Sadie organized a brothel on a road called Virtue Avenue in Kingston and a second brothel plus a fine hotel in Hillsboro. She married a man named Orchard and helped him run the local stage line, legendarily driving the teams herself. She also passed the hat in the saloons for the construction of a church and tended the sick and dying during epidemics. She fought the move of the county seat to Palomas Hot Springs (T or C) in 1938, where she was contradictorily buried in 1943. Hillsboro is today a quiet artist and writer's retreat.

As the mining boom lost momentum around 1893, settlers brought in by mines and associated interests began looking for places to put down roots. One place they looked to was Hot Springs. The town of Hot Springs began as a bathhouse built by cowboys from the Bar Cross and John Cross Ranches in 1882. The adobe shack sheltered a mineral springs in the middle of what was then only a *bosque* (grove) and *tule* (bulrush) swamp next to the river. The Bar Cross Ranch was headquartered at Engle (first spelled Engel), the capital of the Jornada. Engle had served as a freighting supply station for the mining district and later as a shipping station on the AT&SF Railroad.

The exact location of the Cross Ranch bathhouse is not confirmed. One story says the Cross Ranch bathhouse was erected in 1895 west of the hill where the Vera Hotel had stood at its final location. Still another story places the Cross shelter near the Engle ferry. Stagecoaches, light rigs, livestock, soldiers, and people were shuttled across the Rio Grande on a flat-bottomed boat operated by rope and cable. The ferry was the only means of crossing the river for a hundred miles, and its location depended on the flow of the river, but it was usually stationed near Fort McRae. Engle's ford has also been described as a stationary location where the Rio Grande plunges into the Caballo Mountains and veers sharply to the left. This later became the site of the Elephant Butte Dam.

In 1884, the newly established Sierra County appropriated $400 to improve the Geronimo's Spring bathhouse, and a photograph shows this to be the site of the original Cross Ranch bathhouse. One story has it that soldiers from Fort McRae had expanded the hole for this spring. The improved spring was described as an open pool rocked up around the sides. The water bubbled up from the sand in the bottom of the pool and overflowed into the slough and then to the river (which at that time was nearby). Later, this was replaced with two cement tubs that could be drained and refilled. Today, the public can visit these springs on Main Street next to the Geronimo Springs [sic] Museum. The waters flow from a rock fountain sheltered by a cement-block structure with open Moorish archways.

Determining the location of some place names is impeded by the construction of Elephant Butte Dam, which drastically altered the appearance of McRae Canyon. Fort McRae is now under the waters of Elephant Butte Lake. After the completion of Caballo Dam below Elephant Butte in 1938, the lake waters began to rise and undermine some of the foundations of the Spanish community of Las Palomas, and a few families and businesses moved their structures to higher ground across the highway or escaped to other communities.

Other disturbances to historical data were occurrences of flash floods, which destroyed a good number of communities in this area and forced the people to relocate. The Rio Grande flowed down what is now Main Street past Geronimo's Spring. One text says government workers surveyed and filled in the swamp and marshlands adjoining the springs, thus diverting the river's course. Other texts say that debris from the flood of 1907 caused by a violent cloudburst turned the channel.

Once the river shifted, the area around the bathhouses filled in with numerous hotels and residential establishments to house people seeking cures. Fount Sullivan was the first to file an official homestead claim in 1910. Until then, he had temporarily blocked the Cross Cattle Company from acquiring lands around the springs. Sullivan had been the original postmaster of Monticello in 1881. A freighter from New York, Sullivan changed the town's name from Cañada Alamosa to Monticello to honor his hometown.

In 1911, a construction camp was set up to house and supply workers of the Elephant Butte Dam. As the dam grew so did the fortunes of Palomas Hot Springs. By 1913, the town had a barber shop, two hotels, two saloons, a garage, and a school tent for eight pupils. Otto

Elephant Butte

Goetz brought in one of the first stores and formed the chamber of commerce. Engle, still on the railroad, also prospered as the major supplier of construction materials and operated several bus lines on an improved road down into Palomas Hot Springs. The Lone Star Stage Line, operating between Engle and Hot Springs via Elephant Butte Dam, boasted "the oldest dam drivers and best dam cars on the dam line." Fare was $3 one way.

The dam was completed in 1916, the year Palamos Hot Springs incorporated. Many of the people as well as the barracks and mess halls were moved to Hot Springs. The Vera Hotel was dismantled and floated downriver to the town, and around 1920, it was the first to install a long-distance telephone. When a call came in, the owner called out the name over a megaphone and whoever heard it, passed the message along to the appropriate party. The Vera was converted into office space and was only recently razed. Residents of T or C had grown so used to this landmark that when I informed one that it was no longer there, she said, "Oh, I guess I hadn't seen it for a while."

Mail was delivered to Palomas Hot Springs twice a week on horseback by 1915. The public picked up their mail from a cigar box in Mr. McMillan's store. The *Hot Springs Herald* was founded in 1916 and folded before Christmas of the same year. Reportedly, it was established for an election campaign.

Prior to 1916, "Burro Jim" Hawkins hauled water in barrels on a wagon and sold it for a nickel a bucket. (Children knew not to drink the mineral water and saved their pennies.) A water system was developed, and the first fire plug was installed on Main Street. The large waterwheel, located on East Riverside Drive, hoisted water into a trough and then pumped it into the tank on top of Water Tower Hill. An attractive mural called "Journey to the Sacred Springs" is of Apaches on horseback and adorns the present water tank.

A.H. Hilton, father of hotel tycoon Conrad Hilton, chartered the First National Bank of Hot Springs in 1917. Conrad Hilton (1887-1979) was born and raised in San Antonio, New Mexico, fifty-six miles north of Hot Springs. He and his seven siblings lived and worked in the family hotel in San Antonio. Hilton was educated at the New Mexico School of Mines and became a member of the New Mexico House of Representatives (1912-13). In 1919, after his father's death, Hilton started his chain with the Mobley Hotel in Cisco, Texas. San Antonio is a one-stop-light town and home of the world-famous Owl Bar green-chile cheeseburger, and it is said that Hitlon returned there every year to celebrate his birthday.

It was through Governor Clyde Tingley's relationship with President Franklin D. Roosevelt that the state is now graced with a good number of WPA buildings. The Carrey Tingley Hospital for Crippled Children, built in 1937, is one such project. A couple of years earlier, Tingley had casually mentioned during a visit to Hot Springs that the mineral waters would aid in the treatment of infantile paralysis. The local newspaper quoted the governor on its front page, and two years later, Hot Springs had its hospital (which was moved to Albuquerque in the 1980s). Another prime WPA building is the 1939 post office on Main, with its dramatic impressionistic mural of a Native American coyote shape-shifter painted by Borin Deutich in 1940.

The town's interest in helping arthritis patients coupled with a touch of eccentricity led to a name change in 1950. The national radio program known as *Truth or Consequences* started the American Heart Association with a $1.5 million "Walking Man Contest" and raised millions of dollars for the March of Dimes, Cancer Society, and the Arthritis Foundation, among other health agencies. The show, which began in 1940, had earned a reputation for its wacky stunts and "consequences" that had taken players to the English Channel and the North Pole. In one prank, two contestants, starting on opposite coasts with one half of a thousand-dollar bill in hand, had to travel across the country shouting the name "Heathcliff" in Chinese restaurants to find the other half. Ralph Edwards was the host of the show and was somewhat wacky himself. He was born at 9:13 on Friday the thirteenth in April, 1913, in a Merino, Colorado, farmhouse. To celebrate its tenth anniversary, the show began looking for a publicity stunt that would tie in with its philanthropic nature.

One of the writers came up with the idea of persuading a town to change its name to that of the show. Telegrams were sent to major Western towns, and five answered affirmatively. A writer from *This is Your Life* contacted a reporter in Santa Fe, who suggested they call the state senator in Hot Springs, who was looking for a way to distinguish his town from other health resorts in the country named "Hot Springs." In a special election, the town's residents voted—twice—by a margin of four to one to change the name. (Two more elections were held in the coming years, but the name stuck.) Once it became official, the nearby town of Williamsburg changed its name to Hot Springs, and years later, reclaimed the first identity which had been originally selected to honor a local physician.

Producer Jack Bailey set up the radio broadcast from the high-school auditorium on, when else, April Fool's Day. A subsequent two-part program of the television version of *Truth or Consequences*, which can be viewed at the Geronimo Springs Museum, was shot at the rodeo grounds. During the show, a woman was challenged to bridle a horse for a Tappan gas range. A cowboy had to work out a math problem while staying on a bucking bronco for a $200, windproof, golden

Zippo lighter. Ralph Edwards himself rode around on a miniature burro and was pushed in a barrel by a steer. The program was ironically sponsored by Phillip Morris, which made a sizeable donation to the state Arthritis Foundation.

Thus began a love affair between the town and Mr. and Mrs. Edwards. Anniversary celebrations of the show turned into an annual fiesta the first weekend every May, and Ralph and Barbara Edwards have come to every one. Celebrity guests attending the event have included Tab Hunter, Tex Williams, Jane Mansfield, Mollie Bea, Rose Marie, Peter Graves, Ann B. Davis, Kathie Lee Johnson (Gifford), Alejandro Rey, Andy Devine, Fabian, The Hagars, Wayne Newton, and Richard Dawson. The Ralph Edwards Wing in the Geronimo Springs Museum features fiesta memorabilia and an ode to the name change. The Ralph Edwards Riverside Park, a few blocks southeast of the museum, offers sheltered picnic tables, a gazebo, and a fish pond.

A centerpiece of the Geronimo Springs Museum is a skull from a wooly mammoth found in the mid-Rio Grande Valley. Other rooms follow the history of the local forts, mining camps, cattle towns, construction of the dam, as well as historic and prehistoric Indian artifacts. Bronze figures and murals by a local sculptor and artist feature: Spanish explorer Juan de Oñate, Geronimo, Mexican revolutionary Pancho Villa, and cowboy novelist Eugene Manlove Rhodes, who had worked on the Aleman Ranch.

Callahan's Auto Museum is a must-see. The museum exhibits more than three thousand pieces of automobile memorabilia, antique and contemporary car toys and models, antique maps, and car books. Fire had closed the museum temporarily when Andrew and I were there, but the polished vintage cars and trucks parked in front are delightful.

A number of interesting shops are within walking distance of the Geronimo Springs Museum, between Main and Broadway. There are a dozen or more restaurants to enjoy in T or C and Elephant Butte. Quite by serendipity, I stumbled into an interesting eating establishment called the Blue Note Cafe at 407 Broadway. The Blue Note is owned by former Las Cruces morning radio deejay Jim "the Jimster" Brennan with his brothers and mother, Ida. Originally from upstate New York, with time spent in Seattle, the three brothers loved jazz, wanted to play jazz, and desired to start a recording label under the name of their favorite jazz club known as the Blue Note. Well, they all ended up in the Truth or Consequences/Las Cruces area and started a business playing records at dances and weddings under the license of Blue Note. When it was decided to put their forty-three years of combined cooking experience (their day jobs) to work in a cafe, they switched over the license. The restaurant features the food they miss from New York and Seattle, like Buffalo wings, Italian pasta dishes, and subs. They also serve luxurious salads and such Blue Note classics as Chicken Parmesan and Steak Marsala with linguini on the side. They say T or C is a "cultural anomaly," but it is they who are the anomaly.

At temperatures between 98 and 115 degrees Fahrenheit, the springs carried a reputation for centuries for curing ailments affecting the muscles and joints. Drinking the water was believed to aid the digestive system. In the 1930s to 1950s, hundreds came to see Magnolia (Yoakum) Ellis at the bathhouse by the same name for her uncanny ability to heal with her hands. Believers can still partake of the mineral waters at five modern bathhouses for about $2 for up to twenty minutes or can sit in the multitude of undeveloped springs au naturale, if one knows where to look. Most of the houses are registered with and licensed by the state of New Mexico and offer individualized tubs or family-sized pools, as well as other health services, such as massages. The pH of the water is about seven, or neutral, and contains no odor. In addition to the mineral analysis below, there is also a small percentage of radium in the water, considered one of the most healing elements known.

Water Analysis

MINERAL	PARTS PER MILLION
Sodium Chloride	1,771.6
Potassium Chloride	131.4
Potassium Nitrate	0.8
Bicarbonate	278.6
Calcium Chloride	143.9
Calcium Sulfate	113
Silica	43
Alumina	3.2
Iron Carbonate	0.6
Chloride	63.1
Total Solids	2,459.2

Source: Water and Beverage Laboratory, Bureau of Chemistry, Department of Agriculture.

Of course, the hundreds of thousands who flock to Elephant Butte Lake State Park every summer believe those waters to be curative. Named for the pachyderm formation peeking out of the waters at the south end of the lake, it is the largest in the state with thirty-eight thousand acres of surface water and two hundred and fifty miles of sandy beaches. The lake is known for its black and white bass, catfish, and pike, and the park plants crappie and trout in the river below the dam. Water skiing is popular in the months between April and September, and camping facilities provide year-round enjoyment. Having camped and boated at the lake numerous times during my college days, I always found the winter months to be less crowded and cooler to downright chilly. My neighbors, Dave and Jacie Jensen, own the ice business in the Elephant Butte/T or C area and do quite well in the summer, especially around the holidays. There's a spectacular fireworks display on the lake during the Fourth of July celebration. Showers, modern restrooms, and portable toilets are placed at strategic locations. Houseboats moor at the several marinas. Rock Canyon Marina has handicap facilities and a wheelchair ramp.

Elephant Butte is a town with a number of motels, restaurants, grocery stores, and supply stores, and golfing is nearby. The dam site south of the butte is a full-service recreational area with a dining room, lounge, dancing at night, shops, cabins, RV park on the water, and a marina. Although the terrain makes the dam site seem deceptively isolated, it is only five minutes from downtown Truth or Consequences.

For more information:

(Addresses are in Truth or Consequences, NM 87901)
Geronimo Springs Museum, 505-894-6600
Callahan's Auto Museum, 505-894-6900
Chamber of Commerce, 505-894-3536 or 800-831-9487
Blue Note Cafe, 505-894-6680
Artesian Bath House and RV Park, 505-894-2684
The Charles Motel and Bath House, 505-894-7154
Indian Springs Apartments and Pools, 505-894-3823
Sierra Grande Lodge and Health Spa, 505-894-6976

Additional information:

Dam Site Restaurant, Lounge, Cabin Reservations,
    Elephant Butte, NM 87935, 505-894-2073
Elephant Butte State Park,
    Elephant Butte, NM 87935, 505-744-5421
Ice Company Enterprises, Elephant Butte, NM 87935,
    505-744-4119

Directions:

From Las Cruces in southern New Mexico, take exit Interstate 40 off of Interstate 10, turn south and go one mile on New Mexico Route 28. From New Mexico Route 28, turn west on Calle de Santiago or Calle de Parian to arrive at the plaza. Population: 1,975; elevation: 3,857; county: Doña Ana.

Highlights:

Famed church bell, including the Great Bell; San Albino Church; Gadsden Museum; Oliver Lee Memorial State Park; Mesilla Book Center; wonderful restaurants, with hot *chile* (versus chili) sauces; large and small adobe homes; nearby Mount Tortugas; Civil War history.

CHAPTER 7

MESILLA

Caught in the Margins of History

ince the mid-nineteenth century, the town that settled on the *mesilla* (little table land) on the *Río Grande del Norte del Bravo* (Rio Grande), has been a turnstile between several political factions. Within one short decade, Mesilla went from being a Mexican colony for accidental Americans to the capital of the Gadsden Purchase to the capital of the Confederate Territory of Arizona. Until 1881, when the railroad snubbed it in favor of Las Cruces, Mesilla (sometimes romantically referred to as La Mesilla) was the largest commerce and transportation center between San Diego and San Antonio. It was called the jewel of the Southwest and the pearl of Mesilla Valley; it was the scene of Billy the Kid's trial and the sanctuary for Emperor Maximilian. Today, its territorial plaza— buffered by pecan orchards and cotton fields—invites leisurely shopping, dining, and perhaps a *siesta*. Yet for all appearances, this town is definitely not asleep.

The *barrios* of flat-topped adobe homes, inhabited by both the wealthy and the poor, are impressively well maintained. Even the dirt looks as if swept by a straw broom. Strict zoning ordinances prohibit pay phones and gas stations in and around the historical plaza. Until the 1980s, there were no street signs, and that's because the streets weren't named. To keep the city of Las Cruces from swallowing the village, the board of trustees limited development in the greenbelt rural area to single-family homes on five-acre lots. It has been a trade-off. The zoning undermines those natives who traditionally subdivide their tracts and annex their homes for aging parents or returning children and their families. Although zoning has been a hot potato at public meetings in the past couple of decades, certain savvy developers have begun to chip away at this greenbelt.

Just as it takes friction to polish a gemstone, political tension is what gives the town of Mesilla its luster. The summer we visited, a *Las Cruces Bulletin* reporter acknowledged her surprise when a public meeting over a smoking ordinance never erupted into the fiery debate that was expected. While ducking in and out of the shops and the church (both well worth the trek), I repeatedly heard about these issues. I was laughed at when I confessed that I was yet another writer attempting to capsulize Mesilla and then was told whose historical claims were accurate and whose weren't and whose were inflated. Apparently, power here depends upon one's genealogical link to, or knowledge of, the past.

Mesilla's long history of political divisiveness began after the Mexican War (1846-48) when the treaty of Guadalupe Hidalgo dictated the Rio Grande as the boundary between Mexico and the United States. Spanish settlers of Doña Ana Colony on the American (east) side of the river waded across to the other side to remain under Mexican rule. The settlers received land in 1853 from the Mexican government under the Mesilla Civil Colony Grant, then in the province of Chihuahua, just in time to lose it to the United States in the Gadsden Purchase.

I say this is when the divisiveness began, but it was actually preceded by the settlement of the Pueblo village of Tortugas (turtles) just south of Mesilla. Some anthropologists believe the villagers are descendants of Indians expelled from Isleta del Sur, south of El Paso. That pueblo was settled by families who were taken from the original Isleta Pueblo south of Albuquerque by Governor Otermín when he fled to El Paso after the Pueblo Revolt of 1680. According to local tradition, the weak and aged who could travel no farther were dropped off near Mesilla, and they founded Tortugas. The village is divided into the San Juan and Guadalupe sections. Nearby Mount Tortugas indeed looks like a turtle and is the scene of an annual procession of torches commemorating the three appearances of Mexico's patron saint, Our Lady of Guadalupe, to the Indian Juan Diego on a hill outside Mexico City on December 10 to 12, 1531.

While the exact borders of New Mexico and Arizona were being debated in 1850, lobbyists for the southern route of the Pacific Railroad pressured the government to buy the disputed border of Mexico to provide right of way for their projected line. American diplomat James Gadsden was sent to buy 45,535 square miles for $15 million, but at the last minute, the U.S. Senate decided this was not a bargain and instead offered a treaty whereby Mexico ceded a rectangular strip of about thirty thousand square miles in the Mesilla Valley for $10 million. The treaty was consummated with the raising of an American flag on the Mesilla plaza November 16, 1854. Unhappy Mesilleros fled south of the border.

The United States government encouraged stage and freight services from coast to coast, and in 1857, Mesilla became a central point on the Butterfield Overland Mail route between Missouri and California. Those who wagered that the coach from the west would reach Mesilla ahead of the coach from the east won. Headquarters and stage stop were set up in what are now El Patio and La Posta restaurants. Anglo merchants, including Sam and (Judge) Roy Bean, who had set up shop to supply Fort Fillmore near Mesilla in 1851, really began to prosper from the new freighting industry.

Meanwhile, Arizona, New Mexico, and Texas continued to play tug o'war with the territorial borders, compromising on several different territorial configurations in the decade following the end of the Mexican War. At one point, New Mexico included all of the present state of Arizona, to its dissatisfaction, and portions of Colorado and Nevada. In 1857, it was proposed that New Mexico include the northern half (above the 34th parallel) of the two states combined and Arizona the southern half.

Enter the opportunistic Confederate Colonel John Robert Baylor and 220 Texas Mounted Troops. In July, 1861, five hundred troops garrisoned at Fort Fillmore surrendered to Baylor following a skirmish. Baylor, headquartered on the site of the present Fountain Theatre in Mesilla, proclaimed himself military governor and Mesilla the capital of the new territory of Arizona for the Confederacy. In 1863, Congress established the boundary between New Mexico and Arizona where it is today at the 32nd meridian, and subsequent surveys and bills fixed the borders with other states. Mind you, New Mexico was not to become a state until 1912.

An uneasy quiet prevailed over Mesilla during the year the Confederates were in control. When rebel troops had fled back to Texas by July 1862, so did supporters who abandoned their property. The California Column, a Union army composed of fourteen hundred troops and civilian employees, began arriving in the valley. Mesilla returned to its enterprises, but that wasn't the end of the political rivalry.

Just before the 1871 election, Republican and Democratic parties had decided to hold meetings on the plaza on the same day in August. Foreseeing trouble, the heads of the two parties scrambled to hold their meetings peacefully in separate locations. One of the political groups decided it would be fitting to end the day by marching around the plaza which is not very big. Not to be outdone, the other party began marching in the opposite direction. The two collided in front of Reynolds and Grigg's store on the plaza (which today houses the renowned Mesilla Book Center). The bloody riot left nine dead and forty or fifty wounded. Many Republican families, the liberals of their day, abandoned their homes and moved to Mexico. Some returned in later years to become important players in future elections.

The Rio Grande divided Las Cruces and Mesilla at first, but the two cities were joined by a ferry. The great flood of 1863 cut a second channel west of Mesilla, making it a malaria-infested island until the channel chose the western route in 1865, and that left a drying river bed between the town and Las Cruces. Still later, Mesilla fought two more losing battles with Las Cruces, one to get the railroad, the other to retain the county seat.

Mesilla then began to drift slowly into rural obscurity while Las Cruces eventually developed into New Mexico's second largest metropolitan area. In the late 1950s, a suggestion that Las Cruces annex Mesilla led the latter town to incorporate. This is when trustees approved zoning ordinances to preserve the historic architecture and limit development. Fears increased in the 1960s when Mesilleros saw a Territorial-era church in downtown Las Cruces razed to become a vacant lot. At about the same time, urban-renewal projects destroyed much of Las Cruces's adobe and brick business district and replaced Main Street with a mall. Since then, courtroom and political fights have centered on attempts to subdivide and develop farmlands, on who controls the town plaza and how to restore it, whether to allow pitched-roof homes in the historic district, and whether New Mexico Route 28 should be widened through town.

When Andrew and I visited Mesilla in the summer of 1995, land was being leveled for a new subdivision on the old river bed, and tar was being layered on the newly widened New Mexico Route 28. The activity could be heard while inside the nearby Gadsden Museum. Curator Mary Veitch Alexander said the vibrations from the heavy equipment were cracking the walls. She is one person dismayed by these signs of progress, vowing that she would never leave the Gadsden Museum (operated in her ancestral home) to Mesilla for fear of what happened in Las Cruces.

The museum is dedicated to Mary Alexander's great-grandfather, Colonel Albert Jennings Fountain. Fountain entered New Mexico with the First California Volunteer Infantry in 1862 and was stationed at Fort Fillmore, during which time he courted a descendant of Cervantes, Mariana Perez, who became his future bride and mother of his nine children. (Later, his company fought Apaches and helped establish Fort McRae at Ojo del Muerto. See Truth or Consequences Chapter.) During his lifetime, he was a Texas state senator, Speaker of the House in the New Mexico territorial legislature, a newspaper publisher, playwright, district attorney, and the trial lawyer who defended Billy the Kid for the murder of Sheriff William Brady in 1881— he lost. He led the Mesilla Militia in repeated campaigns against the Apaches, and his unit of cow-pony vigilantes so impressed Theodore Roosevelt that he patterned his Rough Riders after them. In 1896, Fountain mysteriously disappeared with his young son, Henry, near Chalk Hill between the Organ Mountains and present-day White Sands. His Masonic pin, ripped from his coat, wasn't returned to the family until 1949, but the bodies were never found.

Fountain's political career is again reflective of the divisiveness in Mesilla, which is only a microcosm of New Mexico's politics. When

Fountain won a close election as a Republican for a seat in the territorial house of representatives, he made an enemy of Democratic candidate Albert Bacon Fall, a Kentucky-born rancher. (Fall was later to become a key figure as Secretary of Interior in the Teapot Dome Scandal.) Fountain was hired by the ranchers' association to prosecute cattle rustling, and the smaller ranchers, consisting of mostly Democrats, saw this as harassment since their growth depended upon picking up strays. Fall became outspoken in the partisan issue, and his associate, Oliver M. Lee, was also accused of rustling. When in January of 1896 Fountain disappeared, he was returning from serving indictments on Lee and thirty-one others at the Lincoln courthouse.

Pat Garrett (the man who shot Billy the Kid at Fort Sumner in 1881) was called out of retirement to round up Lee, whose ranch was near the site where Fountain disappeared, and Lee's friend John Gililland. After two years of an embarrassingly unproductive pursuit, Republican Governor Miguel Otero created a new county that included Chalk Hill, thereby removing it from Garrett's jurisdiction and relieving the political tension and honoring himself with the new county in his name. Lee and Gililland surrendered to the new county sheriff and were acquitted of Fountain's murder at the 1899 trial in Hillsboro for lack of evidence and bodies. Attorney for the defense was none other than Albert Fall, and he made no deathbed confessions at the end of his life.

Oliver Lee went on to build a ranching empire. His fame was such that after his death the Oliver Lee Memorial State Park was established, a fact that does not delight the Fountain family. Three hundred descendants of the main players in this tragedy, mainly involving five families, met in Hillsboro in February, 1996, on the centennial of Fountain's disappearance. It was the first time members of these families had spoken to each other civilly, though sentiments were only slightly diminished by the passage of generations.

A simple marker, six miles north of Las Cruces, commemorates the spot where Garrett was shot in the back in 1908. He was buried in Las Cruces' Odd Fellows Cemetery at Compress and Brown Roads. The Garrett family moved his remains to a larger plot across the street

Mesilla gift shop is the old courthouse where
Billy the Kid was tried and sentenced

in the Masonic Cemetery in 1957 where his wife and seven of their eight children are interred.

Fountain owed his political foot-up to his in-laws, one of them being Antonio Garcia, another great-grandfather to the present owner of the Gadsden Museum. Garcia and his brother were among Republicans who moved to La Ascension, Mexico, after the political riot on the Mesilla Plaza in 1871. A bullet dented the bugle he wore during the rally, and it now hangs in the museum. The Garcia brothers were gone three years during which time they lived on milk, corn, and beans and taught the people how to make farm equipment and to build homes. Upon their return to La Mesilla, they reestablished the Republican party and won the second election.

Upon his father's death, Albert J. Fountain Jr. took up painting to keep from going insane. A replica of his painting of the signing of the Gadsden Purchase is in the Smithsonian and is the centerpiece of the Gadsden Museum, which displays many of his other paintings, including a self-portrait and character studies of famous Southwestern tribal leaders. That's his mural depicting valley scenes on the outer wall of the Fountain Theater on Calle de Nuestra Señora de Guadalupe, established in 1905. The theater now hosts wine tastings, film festivals, chamber music, and plays.

The house that holds the Gadsden Museum three blocks east of the plaza was built in 1860 by Anastacio and Rafarla Barela and enlarged in 1875 by Sheriff Mariano Barela for his mother. When the sheriff died in 1892, the house was turned into a commune with separate families owning each room. When in 1925 Albert Fountain Jr. bought the house, an Indian named Simon Urbina charged $3000 for his single room as compensation for taking care of the invalid Mrs. Barela.

The Gadsden Museum is open Monday through Saturday from 9:00 A.M. to 5:00 P.M. with a two-hour lunch break, and Sundays from 1:00 P.M. to 5:00 P.M. It is like grandma's attic and is actually the accumulation of five generations of family mementos. "My people were hoarders and I thank God for that," said Mary Alexander. For about $2.00 plus tax, Mary locks the front door behind a handful of people and gives them an item-by-item tour. Newcomers who ring the doorbell join the tour in progress and then are given the opportunity to catch the beginning of the tour, like a continuous play-back loop. Mary took over this job in 1972 from her uncle and aunt, Aureliano and Elizabeth Fountain Armendariz, who founded the museum in 1952. Living in a museum is tough; there's no privacy, no closet space, and electrical wires are everywhere. But "God put us where he wanted us and he gave us our people," she says. "Whatever we take out of this life, we have to put back into it."

The museum holds an unusual collection of dolls (one has three faces that rotate to show different emotions), clay marbles, political buttons, medals, old flags and maps, Indian artifacts and bones, irons, clothes, pottery, baskets, a 1602 document chest from Spain, and the 1901 book of presidential portraits signed by each president. Republicans to the end, Mary has an extensive collection of elephants. The Sisters of Mercy taught Mary's mother to decorate china with mother-of-pearl in-lay and there are samples of that in the museum. In the backyard there's a replica of the jail (with the original bar doors) that had held Billy the Kid in 1881 while he stood trial and awaited his sentencing. (See Lincoln and Fort Sumner Chapters.) Juan Maria Justiniani (also known as Giovanni María d'Agostino) is another character who comes to life in the museum. A penitent known as "The Hermit," he was famous for his faith healing, gift of prophecy, and unusual life that ended at La Cueva, the cave in the Organ Mountains where he lived, prayed, and was murdered. Born in Italy, he traveled through South America, Mexico, and Canada before arriving in New Mexico in 1863 and later installed himself in the mountains near Mesilla. As penance, the Hermit wore a belt of spikes and slept on a bed of straw, thorns, and thistles covered only by a thin blanket. He walked to Mesilla for mass two or three times a week, and he lit a bonfire every Friday night to let Colonel Fountain know he was all right. His cane, bell, religious books, rosaries, crucifix, and diary, are now on display in the museum.

Jose Aragon, a famous New Mexico *santero* from Spain, carved a crucifix that is on display along with other *santos*. The lifelike figure of Christ made of leather and human hair is used by San Albino Church in the candlelit Good Friday procession around the plaza for the Holy Burial (*El Santo Entierro*) as it was used by *penitentes* in Spain more than three hundred years ago. The *santos* collection is located within the family chapel inside the museum, which is still used for mass three or four times a year.

The Catholic Church has been the heart and soul of Mesilla since the *Cura* (administrator) Ramón Ortiz, who served as both priest and Commissioner of Emigration, established the colony on the west bank of the Rio Grande from 1849 to 1852. After crossing the river, the colonists pulled their wagons and animals into a rough defensive circle around what was to become the sandy plaza of La Mesilla. They built a tiny chapel, a hut of logs chinked with mud, at the south end. (The church docent said some believe that El Patio restaurant, with its low, rounded bell casing, was the original chapel.) The church was referred to in Spanish records in 1850 as *la iglesia de San Albino*, the church of Saint Aubin. He was the French Bishop of Angers (c. A.D.

550) who ransomed slaves, helped widows and orphans, and was credited with restoring eyesight, healing the sick, and raising the dead on at least one occasion. A church of adobe clay brick was constructed on a foundation of lava rocks on the north end of the plaza in 1855 to 1856 and served as a fortress from Indian attack.

Meanwhile, a contest had developed between the ancient See of Durango and the newly created Bishopric of New Mexico under Jean Baptiste Lamy, a priest of French descent. (See Pecos chapter.) As European ideas gradually replaced the Mexican nature of the church, the building itself underwent a series of cosmetic facades replicating the architectural styles of the French churches. By 1906, the present Romanesque church of San Rafael brick totally replaced the old *iglesia*.

In 1876, the first bell, *Sagrada Corazón de Jesús*, was blessed and was joined by the *María Albina* bell at a later unknown date. The bells were recast and dressed in lacy white baptismal clothes for their new blessing with their attending human *padrinos* (godparents) on August 15, 1886, the Feast of the Assumption. The Great Bell, *Campana Grande*, was dedicated and hung in 1887. The bells still give the town its voice as they ring in the congregation for the daily early-morning mass and for feast days. The task of bell-ringing has traditionally gone to descendants of Manuel Valles of Chihuahua, Mexico, who began ringing the bells in the 1800s. The church is open for public viewing from 1:00 P.M. to 3:00 P.M. daily except Sunday.

Feast days are celebrated on the plaza, but probably one of the most important fiestas is the September 16th celebration commemorating the date in 1821 when a Roman Catholic priest and Mexican rebel, Miguel Hidalgo, declared Mexico's autonomy from Spain. Since the event happened so close to Mesilla's founding date, the fiesta celebrated the town's heritage as well as the harvest. Residents stopped conducting this particular fiesta in the early 1970s, but town officials and merchants belonging to the Old Mesilla Association revived it in 1987.

A parade of mariachi bands, fiesta royalty, mounted *vaqueros* (cowboys and the sheriff's posse), and town officials on floats wind past pecan orchards, chile fields, and homes. Some of the floats carried Indian and Mexican themes featuring, for instance, the Aztec king

Moctezuma in plumage and gilt loincloth. Ballet *folklorico* and other groups perform traditional Mexican *rancheras* dances on the plaza. The festivities are much tamer than in the old days when people came to Mesilla from miles around for *bailes* (dances) and fiestas, bull- and cockfights, and drama and burlesques at the Mesilla Opera House once located on the northwest corner of the plaza.

The year 1881 froze in time in Mesilla, for the buildings on the plaza look much as they did then. There is a *Historic Walking Tour of Mesilla* available for about $4.25 (or less, depending on where you buy it). Information in the booklet is not completely accurate according to the locals and my own brief experience, but it offers a flavor of Mesilla's door-to-door history and a glimpse of people plus a few of the ghosts behind those doors.

The Town of Mesilla and the Old Mesilla Association distribute an attractive map of the shops and restaurants on the plaza. The Mesilla Book Center features the best selection of Southwestern rare and out-of-print books I have ever seen. Other shops around the plaza offer clothing, fine art, jewelry, crafts, and souvenirs to fit every taste and pocketbook. Most of the buildings are owned by the original family lines, which speaks for the tenacity and longevity of Mesilla's core residents.

On the southeast corner of the plaza is the William Bonney Gallery in the old territorial courthouse and jail. (Cartoonish Western Characters peer over the saloon doors painted onto the regular storefront doors.) This was the site of Billy the Kid's two-day trial in April, 1881. The building was built in the 1850s and was a store from 1859 until after the Civil War when the county acquired it for use as a courthouse and jail. When the county seat was moved to Las Cruces in 1882, Florecio Lopez operated the Elephant Butte Saloon and Billiard Parlor in it until around 1913. It is now owned by Tito Lucero. Gallery owners Dan and Della McKinney had purchased the La Tienda gift shop next door from one of Dan's high-school teachers in 1975. Dan happened to have mentioned to the teacher that he would be interested in the shop someday, and she said she couldn't let him have it in January, but maybe in February. The gallery features fine native American crafts including an extensive collection of pottery by artisans of Casas Grandes, Mexico.

Visitors can literally eat their way around the plaza in such shops as Going Nuts at Mesilla, J. Eric Chocolatier, and Adelina's Pasta Shop. Besides El Patio Restaurant and Cantina, owned and operated by Albert Jennings Fountain (the fifth), there's the Double Eagle and Peppers. The Double Eagle, once the Confederate governor's mansion and rumored to be inhabited by ghosts, was redecorated and furnished with antiques and ornate gold-leaf mirrors. It shares space with Peppers, a more casual restaurant decorated with a Southwestern flair to match its colorful menu. And then there's La Posta.

I don't know how old I was when I first ate at La Posta as a kid. At that time, the plaza and the roads of Mesilla were all dirt, but very little if anything has changed about the restaurant. Andrew was more impressed by the tropical birds in the patio areas than the fact that one has a choice of dining in a number of rooms that catered to the old Butterfield Stage Lines: the freight depot (now a party room), the tannery, the saddle shop, the harness room, the school room, the lava room lined with volcanic rock, or the winery room from where the Gallegos family supplied sacramental wine to the churches of the Rio Grande Valley. Opened in 1939 by Katy Camuñez Meek, the Mexican cuisine from old family recipes were praised in *Life*'s July 1957, issue, and the restaurant is still getting a lot of mileage out of that one.

To most New Mexicans, red *chile* is the blood of their life, and green *chile* the light. I once asked a transplant from North Dakota if she had become addicted to the hot chili yet. She shrugged and said she had tried it before, thinking I was referring to Texas chili (spelled with the traditional "i") with meat and beans. I asked her which she preferred, red or green, and she said, "It comes in a color?" The arid, hot Mesilla Valley is best known for its green chili, particularly from the town of Hatch forty or so miles northwest of Mesilla. Red chili, which is actually the color of a ripe chili pepper (most of us can't wait for it to turn), is best purchased in Chimayo, New Mexico, north of Santa Fe. I leave it open for debate. The chili industry was started in the Mesilla Valley in the early 1900s, and today southern New Mexico harvests twenty-eight thousand acres of the vegetable with a cash value of nearly fifty million dollars.

Historians believe the Pueblo Indians grew the chili pepper as early as the 1850s, although it may have been cultivated by the Maya-Toltec-Aztec culture in the Valley of Mexico centuries earlier and imported to New Mexico by Spaniards. Different varieties of the hot peppers have been bred at New Mexico State University in Las Cruces. A chili pepper is a member of the nightshade family, and although rich in vitamins A and C, the active ingredient, capsaicin, is addictive. But don't let that stop you from perusing the chili stands along New Mexico Route 28 near the Mesilla plaza.

The following recipe for green-*chile* enchiladas (or *enchiladas verdes*) is adapted from La Posta's recipe book, but it is actually in the public domain:

12 green chili peppers
 2 medium tomatoes or 1 medium-sized can
    stewed tomatoes
 1 medium onion, chopped
 2 small garlic cloves, minced or
    a teaspoon of garlic powder
 1 teaspoon salt
    water
 1 dozen corn tortillas
 2 cups grated cheese
    (usually cheddar or Monterrey Jack or both)
 3 cups green chili sauce (commercial brand)

Roast chili peppers directly over electric or gas burner or barbecue grill until outside skin can be easily peeled. (Note: Most people freeze bags of pre-roasted chili peppers and then peel what is needed for each meal. If you don't wear gloves and you burn your hands on the seeds, I have found that coating hands with granulated sugar subdues the sting. Hatch and Bueno are

good store-bought chili brand substitutes.) Remove
core, seeds and visible veins of the chili pepper. Chop
into half-inch pieces. Place in saucepan and add tomatoes, onion, salt, and garlic. Add enough water to cover;
simmer ten minutes.

Allow two or three tortillas per person. Fry tortillas in hot fat, quickly immerse in sauce, then build on
plate layer-cake fashion with grated cheese sprinkled
between layers. Pour green chili sauce over stack and
garnish with lettuce.

Local citizen Lionel "Joe Lee" Frietze, whose Sephardic great-grandfather migrated to Mesilla in 1851 from Germany via Texas, tells the
story of the time when Don Julio Mestas, an elder of Mesilla, had
served skunk chili to the *vaqueros* during a cattle roundup. Don Julio
had gone to Mesilla for supplies and was forced to return to camp
without the one ingredient he needed for *chile colorado con carne* (red
chili with meat), which he had promised the men for the evening
meal. He decided he would shoot a rabbit or two for the chili, but he
did not see a rabbit, so he shot a skunk instead. When the vaqueros
returned for their meal, he warned them not to drink water with their
chili, knowing that that would reactivate the perfume. But the chili
was so spicy, one man did reach for the water, and upon drinking it,
realized what he had eaten. If all the stories about quick-draw shoot-
outs were true, Don Julio would have been dead.

Despite the fireworks in this old town, the flavors, scenery, and
hospitality make for a beautiful and, yes, tranquil retreat, especially
between September and May. Mesón de Mesilla on Avenida de Mesilla
is a bed and breakfast and country inn that offers a seasonal pool, a
gourmet restaurant, and wrap-around balconies that view the jagged
Organ Mountains. I came across the Happy Trails Bed and Breakfast
quite by accident while driving through the pecan orchards along
Paisano Road. This Spanish hacienda offers the works for both the
travelers and their horses. Other lodgings and R.V. parks are available along New Mexico Route 28 near Interstate 10.

For more information:

(Addresses are in Mesilla, NM 88046)
Gadsden Museum, 505-526-6293
San Albino Church, 505-526-9349
Mesilla Book Center, 505-526-6220
William Bonney Gallery, 505-526-8275
La Tienda, 505-524-2513
La Posta Restaurant, 505-524-3524
El Patio Restaurante y Cantina, 505-524-0982
Double Eagle Restaurant, 505-523-6700
Mesón de Mesilla, 800-732-6025
Happy Trails Bed and Breakfast, 505-527-8471
The Old Mesilla Association, P.O. Box 1005, Mesilla, NM, 88046

Directions:

Exit Interstate 25 at San Antonio, New Mexico, and head east on U.S. Route 380 through Carrizozo and Capitan. Or exit Interstate 25 at Alamagordo and take U.S. Route 70 east to U.S. Route 54 north; at Tularosa take U.S. Route 70 east through the Mescalero Apache Reservation and turn left at Hondo on U.S. Route 380. From Roswell, drive west on U.S. Route 380, veering northwest at Hondo. Population: 75; elevation: 5,600; county: Lincoln.

Highlights:

A town with beautifully preserved, century-old buildings; an area full of Billy the Kid legends; Old Lincoln Days' celebrations; Museum of New Mexico; the Wortley Hotel; Casa de Patron; Ellis Store & Co. Bed and Breakfast; nearby Tinnie's Silver Dollar Restaurant and Saloon in the old Tinnie Mercantile Company; Museum of the Old West; Mountain Man and Cowboy Encampment.

CHAPTER 8

LINCOLN
Kid Napped in Lincoln

ndrew and I happened to have hit Lincoln during their Old Lincoln Days celebration, and we thought we were seeing the second coming—of Kid Antrim, that is. During the first weekend of every August, a number of men tuck baggy pants inside scuffed boots, cock hats aslant, and don dull expressions. They're masquerading not as Henry McCarty, the homicidal juvenile from (conjecturally) New York City, but as his alias, William Bonney, the legendary Regulator dubbed Billy the Kid by the old-time *Las Vegas Gazette*. The approximation is based on the only ferrotype taken of him and is now on brochures splattered across half the state.

Lincoln isn't exactly a town anymore; it's an antique. A dozen territorial buildings in this old town stood in the crossfire of a three and a half-year merchant's war more than a century ago. Today, the remarkably preserved structures, manicured gardens, and shady porches defy the notion that the decisive five-day gun battle, in which Bonney became a legend, was set here. You can't take out a marriage license in the courthouse or buy groceries in Tunstall's mercantile, but about seventy-five real people live in Lincoln's old houses, and they don't all dress in nineteenth-century clothing, at least not everyday. Some of them will even admit their weariness of Kid mania, but few will hesitate to pass on historical fact and gossip, whether invited to do so or not.

Preservation of Lincoln's architecture began in 1934 when the WPA under the sponsorship of the Chaves County Historical Society restored the old *torreon*, a stone tower fortification in town. Since then, a number of nonprofit, county, and state agencies have dovetailed their efforts to jealously guard their heritage. In 1938, the state purchased the abandoned courthouse, restored it extensively, and opened it as a monument under the auspices of the Museum of New Mexico. The state has since acquired and restored seven more in the following years. In the 1960s, Lincoln became a colony for artists, eccentrics, and connoisseurs of antiquity who restored other buildings. In 1976, a group of wealthy businessmen and natives in nearby Roswell, including oilmen Robert O. Anderson, Pulitzer author Paul Horgan, and President Johnson's portrait artist, Peter Hurd, formed the Lincoln County Heritage Trust to assume the efforts started by the Old Lincoln County Memorial Commission in the 1940s. The Trust owns seven properties including co-ownership of the monument with the state and the Historic Center book store and museum.

By ordinance passed in 1972, residents are urged to check in with the Lincoln Historic Preservation Board for "advice" on building plans and architectural styles. Their businesses must reflect the general aura of the past. While you cannot buy gas in Lincoln, you can stay in one of Lincoln's three inns or b and bs or purchase fine arts and crafts in one of five shops. But there are no curio shops or tacky signs boasting that you-know-who slept where.

A travel writer called Billy the Kid a one-man cash crop, but I didn't see many people getting rich off him. For $4.50, or nothing if you're under seventeen, you can see all the public museums open during the time of year you visit. Fifty cents extra will buy a self-guided map to thirty-nine houses, churches, businesses, and significant vacant lots, most of them dating back to the 1860s and 80s. You can retrace the Lincoln County War and get all the players straight just by going door to door along the town's single road, U.S. Route 380, which is especially fun during Old Lincoln Days. Yes, you can find out where the Kid napped, where he was shot down, and from where he made his infamous last escape. Parking is available across the street from the pageant grounds where the tour begins at the west end of town, although it is best to start at the Historic Center toward the east end. The gift store offers a good selection of books, and the museum across the courtyard has a theater that runs a twelve-minute video on Lincoln County history.

Hispanic subsistence farmers moved their families and possessions in oxen-pulled wagons from villages south of Albuquerque to Bonito Canyon in 1849, according to the video. Soon, several communities sprang up and were collectively referred to as *las placitas del Rio Bonito*, little settlements on the pretty river. Their *jacales* (houses) were constructed of poles driven into the ground and covered with mud. La Placita, the largest settlement, was built around a *torreon*, a circular tower fortification of stone that provided protection from raiding Apaches. More settlers came when Fort Stanton was established in 1855 eleven miles west of La Placita. A *penitente* chapel dedicated to San Juan served small farms up and down Bonito Canyon. Sheep grazed idyllically in the surrounding hills that walk right up to the town.

The Mescalero Apaches, who had signed a treaty with the U.S. government three years earlier, were removed to the original site of Fort Stanton for a short time. After setting out on their own, they were resettled on their reservation thirty miles to the southwest in 1873. Today, they operate the lucrative Inn of the Mountain Gods and ski run, and visitors are welcome at their information center in Mescalero. The Mescaleros are among a number of New Mexico tribes who have operated casinos on their reservations, their legality pending at the publication of this book.

Fort Stanton was deserted and burned by Union forces in 1861 upon the advance of General Henry Hopkins Sibley's Texas troops. Volunteers under Kit Carson rebuilt the fort in 1868, and for thirty years it served as a military post. It became a U.S. Marine Hospital in 1898 for tubercular patients and a school for the mentally disabled in 1966. After Pearl Harbor, the crew of the German luxury liner, *Columbus*, were kept at Fort Stanton. The crew later incised a boulder and presented it as a token of remembrance. It serves to shelter Lincoln's park, which is a tree-enclosed respite below street level.

Inside the fort's safety zone, La Placita boomed. Farmers and merchants provided crops, goods, and services for an exploding population of soldiers and other newcomers. Railroads in the region turned ranches into empires. La Placita became the seat of a new county, and its name was changed to honor President Lincoln. (To answer the most-asked question once and for all: No, Lincoln was not born here, he was not buried here, he never even saw the place.) Within a decade, Lincoln County became the largest in the United States and, inevitably, ethnic and occupational differences boiled up.

The Lincoln County War began over the rivalry between the mercantile stores of John Tunstall and L. G. Murphy who vied for beef contracts with the army and the Mescaleros among others. A former divinity student from Ireland, Murphy first established a store at the fort in 1866, but was kicked off for unscrupulous business practices. English-born Tunstall tried to challenge Murphy's monopoly. Murphy hired a lawyer, Alexander McSween, to collect the insurance money he claimed Tunstall owed him. But McSween became Tunstall's partner, and Murphy accused him of stealing the $10,000. Murphy was friendly with county officials who obliged him with a warrant for Tunstall's arrest. On February 18, 1878, Tunstall was ambushed and killed while riding from his ranch into Lincoln to turn himself in. Bonney, known as Billy the Kid, was among Tunstall's cowboys who witnessed the murder and vowed revenge. He was in for one heck of a fight, for Murphy was backed by his partner, James Dolan (a Union soldier), the sheriff's department, and the Santa Fe Ring, which included many corrupt state officials. On the McSween side stood the powerful cattleman, John Chisum, whose ranch was four miles south of Roswell.

Not everybody took sides. In a 1938 interview for the WPA Writer's Project, Francisco Gomez said he worked for the McSweens at the age of eighteen when Bonney also worked there. Bonney was a likeable fellow, neatly dressed with rather large front teeth. His roan horse was about ten or twelve hands high and followed him around like a dog. He liked to target practice; he could twirl his six-shooter on his finger and hit a can six times before it hit the ground. Gomez accompanied Bonney on one of his missions to run off some tough outlaws who terrorized Lincoln. "When the Lincoln County War broke out, my father did not want to get into it so he made me quit working for the McSweens and come home and stay there."

Annie Lensett fed Bonney several meals when he came to her ranch on the Ruidoso. In a 1930 WPA interview, she said, "...my husband never knew anything about it, for he had warned me not to feed any

Lincoln Casa de Patrón

of the men from either side." But she fed them anyway, feeling so sorry for them.

Bonney and his pals returned to Lincoln April 1, 1878, and ambushed Sheriff William Brady and his deputy from behind Tunstall's store. Built in 1877, it also housed a bank and law office for McSween and Chisum. The wooden shutters were two layers thick with a sheet of metal between them. Today, the museum displays much of the original merchandise the state found neatly packed in straw-filled boxes in the basement. You can see two little crosses in the yard through the window where Tunstall and McSween were buried. In the living quarters there's a hole in the floor where Bonney may have hidden after the shoot-out.

The war raged for three years, and although there were other shoot-outs and ambushes, the decisive Five Day Battle began on the evening of July 14, 1878, when the so-called Regulators took refuge in the McSween house. Murphy and Dolan's men and Lincoln County Sheriff George Peppin and his posse besieged the house for three days. On

July 19, Colonel Nathan Dudley and his troops marched on Lincoln with a Gatling gun and mountain howitzer, thereby tipping the scales to the Murphy-Dolan side.

The house was set afire, and that night, Susan McSween, the servants, and the other family who lived with them were permitted to leave the burning building. Bonney and some men escaped out the back and along the river. At this point, Alexander McSween and two other men stepped out of the house to surrender, but were killed in the confusion. A sign mistakenly marks the lot where the McSween House once stood, but excavations show the house was to the west. Susan McSween established a ranch at White Oaks and became known as the Queen of Cattle.

Shortly after the gun battle, Lew Wallace became territorial governor and he soon declared martial law at Lincoln. Wallace met with Bonney at Squire Wilson's house (marked on the walking tour) and offered to lessen the charges against Bonney if he would stop his war of revenge. Wallace's goal, which he finally accomplished, was to smash the Santa Fe Ring, and one way was to connect them to Lincoln County politics. Bonney refused the deal, but later said Wallace went back on his word. During Wallace's term, his novel, *Ben Hur: A Tale of the Christ*, was published (1880). He resigned as governor the following year.

The famous black Buffalo Soldiers stationed at Fort Stanton patrolled the streets of Lincoln while it was under martial law. By congressional legislation in 1866, the black man was legally allowed the right to serve in the military and the first black foot and horse soldiers of the post-Civil War period (1866-1900) were called Buffalo Soldiers. As many as 12,500 men served in the 9th and 10th Calvary Regiments and the 38th, 39th, 40th, and 41st Infantry Regiments. The nickname, Buffalo Soldiers, was given to the troops as a symbol of strength by Indians who thought the black hair resembled the mane of the buffalo and the soldiers wore thick buffalo coats in the winter. The regimental coat of arms for the 10th Calvary featured the buffalo as its crest. The 9th and 10th Calvary opened the mail and stage routes from San Antonio to El Paso; established law and order in the

Rio Grande Valley; and performed scouting, long-range patrolling, and cross-border operations on reservations. They guarded important mountain passes, water holes, and isolated settlements, generally paving the frontier for future western cities. The 9th Calvary, who served New Mexico between 1875 through 1881, was the most decorated unit in the Army during the Indian Wars period. (See Truth or Consequences chapter.)

Garrett captured Bonney and his gang at Stinking Spring near Fort Sumner in December 1880 and in April, 1881, was brought to trial in Mesilla and convicted of murdering Brady three Aprils earlier (1878); he was sent to await his execution in Lincoln. (See Fort Sumner and Mesilla chapters.) He was held in a two-story adobe, which had started out as L.G. Murphy's & Co. Built in 1873-74, it was known as the Big Store for six years. Murphy's Mess, across the street, had been built in 1872 in anticipation of construction on the Big Store, but over the years, people referred to it by the cook's last name. When the war came, Wortley's hotel filled up with soldiers and lawmen. The store was sold to the county to be used as sheriff's office, jail, and living quarters, and between 1881 and 1913, it served as the courthouse until the new one was completed at Carrizozo, the new seat.

On April 28, 1881, while Bonney sat in jail across the street, Deputy Sheriff Bob Olinger was eating lunch with five prisoners at the Wortley when he heard shots. Bonney killed his guard, Deputy J.W. Bell, and then through the upstairs window, he shot Olinger as he ran across the street. Engraved stone tablets outside mark the place where the two men fell, and you can see the bullet holes in the west wall of the courthouse. This was Billy the Kid's last escape.

In another WPA interview, Daniel Carabajal remembered seeing Bonney leave town the day he killed Olinger and Bell, though he would have only been two years old. "I was uptown playing with some boys just across the street when Billy killed the guards. We hid behind a picket fence and watched Billy ride out of town. We were too scared to go and see the men he had killed, as we were afraid that he would come back and shoot us."

The first weekend of every August since 1940, the locals have put on a folk pageant commemorating the war and Bonney's vengeance and final escape. Many of the players are descendants of participants in the war. Cost is $3, adults; $1, children 6-12. Several performances are given at the pageant grounds all weekend.

Pat Garrett, who happened to have been at nearby White Oaks when Bonney escaped and who later was the one to assassinate him on July 14, 1881, owned the Wortley hotel for two and half months that summer. (See Fort Sumner Chapter.) The original building burned in the 1930s, but in 1960, it was faithfully restored on the same foundation using the same techniques and specifications by rancher Dessie Sawyer of Tatum, New Mexico, at a cost of $100,000. Builders referred to photographs to replicate the building, and some say the remains of the first adobes were used. A modern kitchen and plumbing were added. The eight guest rooms are furnished in the style of the late 1880s. Along the front is a ninety-two-foot porch, partially enclosed for dining. The dining room is one of the only two restaurants in town open to the public. Serving buffet style, this country inn serves simple but exquisitely prepared home cooking. The Stagecoach Cafe next to the courthouse serves Mexican and American food, and for $1.50, you can tour the privately owned Museum of the Old West.

When I lived in Roswell, many years ago, one of my favorite places was the Victorianesque porch that wraps around Tinnie's Silver Dollar Restaurant and Saloon on U.S. Route 70/380 in the Hondo Valley less than fifteen minutes from Lincoln, which provides an alternative for hungry visitors. Tinnie Mercantile Company first opened in 1882 as a general store and post office. A bell tower, massive oak bar, and an ornate 1880s European Music Box contribute to the Territorial charm. The décor also embodies a skylight from an old San Francisco mansion, four stained-glass windows from an El Paso Presbyterian Church, and a Murano glass mosaic of the four seasons found in an old adobe barn. When artist Peter Hurd was alive, he entertained guests in his own private room, called the Polo Room, after his Hondo Valley enterprise. Admittedly, I was a Hurd voyeur, and I would peek in through the small window in the door while he was playing host at the head of the table.

In the opening shoot-'em-up scene of *Young Guns*, based on the Lincoln County War, Emilio Estevez as Billy the Kid says, "Now, I say we stop off at Juan Patrón's house for one jolly big dram and one ginger beer with a dollop of whipped cream." Apparently, Bonney didn't drink liquor or smoke, but he loved to gamble and dance. He was particularly popular at Hispanic *bailes*, and these dances often took place at Patrón's. The house was built prior to 1868, and between 1871 and 1880, the Patrón family operated a store and saloon in the house.

Handsome Juan Patrón, the elected county clerk, became embroiled in the war, and Susan McSween had taken refuge under his roof when her husband was shot and her own house burned. Because of his sympathy toward the McSween faction, Juan was shot in the back by a partner in the Big Store, but he unexpectedly survived the night and went on to become the youngest Speaker of the House in the territorial legislature. In 1880, he moved to Puerta de Luna south of Santa Rosa, New Mexico, to escape the Lincoln turmoil, but was shot by a cowboy at point-blank range. Apparently, in 1879, Bonney awaited his secret meeting at Patrón's with Governor Wallace to turn state's evidence. It can't be said for sure that he ever fell asleep that night because he was serenaded by town supporters.

This thick-walled adobe with its high ceilings and exposed beams is now a bed and breakfast owned by Jeremy and Cleis Jordan, who preserved that gracious Patrón-style hospitality. Step into the Jordan household and you instantly become a member of their extended family, which includes ABC's *Prime Time Live* anchor Sam Donaldson. Donaldson stayed at the b and b while he periodically monitored the building of his house in the adjoining Hondo Valley. He even sent his contractors to the Patrón house to study certain architectural features.

The main house is furnished with Western art, a washboard collection, a grand piano, and handcrafted organ. An accomplished musician, Cleis is known to perform for guests. With a full house and prior arrangements, the Jordans will put on a theme evening, with matching cuisine and music from such countries as France or Germany. Turning everything into enterprise, they sell homemade candy and handmade soaps through their newsletter. Former Houston residents, they opened Casa de Patrón in 1988, modeled after b and bs in England and Scotland (except Americans prefer private baths). The main house has three guest rooms, and a full gourmet breakfast is offered to houseguests. The two casitas are rented by families; one has a kitchenette and the other a refrigerator and coffee maker, and the price includes a continental breakfast. Plenty of yard space for playing. Rumor has it that the ghost of Juan Patrón will occasionally look in on guests.

One of the house specialties is a pancake dish called Dutch Babies. The following recipe feeds six:

> ¼ cup butter (any premium-grade margarine will do)
> 6 eggs
> 1½ cups each of milk and flour
> 10- inch pie pan (cake pans can also be used, but
>   the sloped sides of pie pans are more conducive
>   to puffing)

Preheat oven to 425 degrees; melt butter or margarine in the pan in oven (do not burn). Whirl eggs and milk in blender until well beaten. Add flour to blender and whip for 15 to 20 seconds at high speed. Pour mixture into the hot melted butter and return to oven. Bake for about 25 minutes until puffed and golden. Allow guests to watch while you take it out of the oven. Cut portions and present them on a plate. Guests may top them with combinations of fresh lemon, powdered sugar, syrup of any kind, fresh fruit compote, yogurt or sour cream, or even salsa, or they can eat them plain with salt and pepper. Catch any butter drippings in the bottom of oven with aluminum foil. As with any souffle, Dutch Babies tend to collapse by the time the plate is presented.

While the Patrón house, with its heavy, smooth walls and dark woods, has a Spanish Territorial feel to it, the Ellis house across the street seems more Victorian. I found David Vigil grilling *fajitas* for Old Lincoln Days-goers on the expansive lawn of the Ellis Store and Co. Bed and Breakfast. He told me the original two-room house was built in 1850, and although it has had eight owners, it is the oldest continuously lived-in residence in Lincoln County, not to mention southeastern New Mexico. It has always offered lodging and meals. Ellis purchased it in 1877 and used it as a ranch headquarters, store, and boarding house. A contingent of the McSween forces were stationed here during the Five Day Battle—in fact, says Vigil, the first shot was taken from the roof of the house. The Vigils claim that it was here that Bonney was kept under house arrest while waiting to meet with Governor Wallace. Ellis was paid $64 for Bonney's and Tom O'Falliard's room and board and to stable the horses. The Vigils say they have the court records to prove it.

Dr. James W. Laws turned the property into a tuberculosis sanitorium in 1905. He built ten little huts along the river for tubercular patients. The huts had no glass on the windows winter or summer because it was believed that clean air, diet, and exercise were curative. He moved the grist mill up from the river and decorated it in a manner that would be attractive to nurses from the East. The bathroom still has the original "butt" bath, which Ginny Vigil says is a 1900 forerunner to the French bidet. Over the years, the mill house has been used as a bunk house in the 1930s (wonder what the cowboys thought of the butt bath), artist's establishment in the 1960s, and as an annual retreat for an insurance company called the Woodmen of the World. Today, the Vigils rent out the two-story house to families, and it is ideal for reunions.

The main house has four rooms and a bright great room decorated with antiques. Heating is by woodburning stove in keeping with the historical integrity of the house (except for modern plumbing). The Vigils also serve a gourmet breakfast with herbs and veggies grown from their own gardens. With reservations, they also serve dinner to ten to fourteen guests in the winter, offering a menu of eight ever-varying items. Outdoor weddings and parties are especially popular on their huge lawn and luxurious porch.

Andrew and I met quite a collection of characters while roaming the town's streets during Old Lincoln Days. A man who looked like James Earl Jones in a Buffalo Soldiers uniform was selling T-shirts and granting photo opportunities to anyone who bought one. A little farther on, folks were meandering through a Mountain Man and Cowboy Encampment of sixteen authentic tents and tipis set up in a vacant lot. Tent fanatics do this as a hobby or business and set up their Marquis, Wedge, One-Pole, or Wall Tents at up to eight hundred or nine hundred such encampments in the country as a spin-off trend from the National Muzzle Loading Rifle Association meeting. In most encampments, the tents, clothing, contents, activity, and sales items must pre-date the 1840s, but the Lincoln rendezvous was extended to the 1880s to encompass the Civil War and cowboy era of the area. It is usually the call of the "Booshway" (from *bourgeois*) or the organizer.

Gold miners were operating a booth where for $5 one could pan for gold in a horse trough filled with river mud from the Dry Gulch or the Nogal. I was told that the first authentic gold discovery in the region was in 1865 on a dry gulch above the Helen Rae mines; but the Helen Rae, one of the most profitable in the area, wasn't discovered until 1880. The operators of the booth claimed they had personally discovered an overlooked vein in the old mine they say might prove to be the biggest gold strike in the history of New Mexico. The real gold mine may have been the $5/pan operation.

I also met Cille Dickinson in a gift shop and one of the few wearing standard denim. She said she had rounded up sheep for her father's ranch on the other side of Capitan and rode her horse all through these hills when growing up. Raised in Roswell, she had always wanted to live in Lincoln. She and her husband finally did move to Lincoln just in time for her to deliver her baby there, and for twelve years, hers was the only child. There are problems living here, she says. Lincoln is not an incorporated village, as a population of two hundred and fifty, a policeman, and a mayor are required for that. For now, the county government makes many of the civic decisions within the constraints of the historic-district zoning, much to the disdain of the local residents. "Everybody is just too independent," says Cille.

For more information:

(Addresses are in Lincoln, NM 88388)
Lincoln State Monument, 505-653-4372
Lincoln County Heritage Trust, 505-653-4025
The Wortley Hotel, 505-653-4300
Casa de Patrón, 505-653-4676
Ellis Store & Co, 505-653-6460

Additional information:

Buffalo Soldiers Society of New Mexico, 505-293-6929
Tinnie Mercantile Restaurant and Saloon,
    Tinnie, NM 88351, 505-653-4425
Lincoln County Gold Mining Co.,
    Ruidoso, NM 88345, 505-257-4070
Mountain Man and Cowboy Encampment,
    Ruidoso, NM 88345, 505-257-7158

Directions:

From Santa Fe, drive southeast on Interstate 25 twenty-five miles, exit at the Rowe Interchange 307 and head north on New Mexico Route 63 six miles to Pecos. Alternatively, exit Interstate 25 at Glorietta at mile marker 299 and drive east on New Mexico Route 50 six miles to Pecos. The village of Pecos is two miles north from the Pecos National Historical Park on New Mexico Route 63. Population: 1,012; elevation: 6,800; county: San Miguel.

Highlights:

A town on the Pecos River between the Great Plains and the Sangre de Cristo Mountains; Pecos National Historic Park; Forked Lightning Ranch; birthplace of legendary Montezuma; site of the Civil War's Battle of Glorietta Pass; St. Anthony's Church; Adele's Town & Country Store; Renata's for gourmet cooking; nearby Silvertip Trader.

CHAPTER 9

PECOS

Civil Pecos

ecos sits where the western edge of the Great Plains meets the majestic Sangre de Cristo Mountains with their towering peaks, lush forests, canyons, and rivulets. Visitors from across the country and various parts of the world are lured by the rugged beauty and historic aura. But for all that has passed before its eyes—the demise of an ancient Indian trading empire, the Spanish Conquest, the Santa Fe Trail, a Civil War battle, and the Hollywood jet set—Pecos is a relatively quiet village.

As the only practical route into the Pecos Wilderness, the usual travel and sporting accommodations crowd the junction of Highways 50 and 60, giving the illusion that this is the center of town. But the town proper is situated on the east side of the Pecos River opposite the highway with its back turned protectively away from the general public. Even the St. Anthony of Padua Church, *La Iglesia de San Antonio del Rio Pecos*, faces the river and not the road. "Narrow, torturous streets" around the church are lined with adobe buildings, ancient and new, which remind one of Old Mexico, says the Town & Country Store's handout. "Yet its modern schools, progressive citizens, and huge ranches give striking evidence of the spirit of the New West."

Pivotal to the history of Pecos are the Forked Lightning Ranch and the Pecos Indian Pueblo, after which the town is named. Both lie in the strategic passage through the Sangre de Cristos Mountains. A Folsom point (a leaf-shaped spearhead) dating to 9,000 B.C. found in the area gives some idea of how long this pass has been a thoroughfare for traffic. Groups began living in pit-house dwellings here in the ninth century, and in the 1100s, immigrants began living in haphazard clusters of rectangular rooms of coursed adobe mud. One such site is known by archaeologists as the Forked Lightning Ruin. At its peak, between A.D. 1225 and 1300, this site alone housed hundreds of people.

Perhaps on the theory that there is safety and productivity in numbers, the Forked Lightning people made an orderly exodus up the sandy arroyo and crossed over to where a steep-sided, flat-topped ridge afforded them a view of the great gray-green mountains looming in the north and the clear and cold but shallow stream that flowed a mile to the east. For about a century and a half, generations of the Forked Lightning people joined others in building, abandoning, and building anew their one-storied sandstone dwellings on the ridge. In the fourteenth century they embarked on a monumental community project, building a single, defensible, four- and five-storied apartment complex with six hundred and sixty rooms and twenty-two kivas (round, underground ceremonial rooms). The town became known as *pekush* or *peko*, meaning "a place by the water," which the Spaniards converted to "Pecos", although the Forked Lightening People called themselves Cicuyé. Their location commanded a trade path between the Pueblo farmers of the Rio Grande and the buffalo-hunting tribes on the plains. Becoming economically powerful, they practiced the arts and customs of two worlds.

Then came the Spanish *entrada*. After Francisco Vásquez de Coronado attacked the Zuñi at Hawikku in 1540 (see Zuñi chapter), he sent bold but wary Captain Hernando de Alvarado to Pecos to look for gold. As many as two thousand people sat on the terraced rooftops awaiting the arrival of the Spanish envoy, escorted by Pecos scouts, and welcoming them with gifts and music. El Turco, a Plains Indian captive, led the Spaniards on a wild golden-goose chase to a mythical wealthy city called Gran Quivera on the Plains—that is, until Coronado caught on and had the man strangled. After a bleak winter on the Rio Grande and a few skirmishes with Pecos and other Pueblos, Coronado led his broken army back to Mexico empty-handed, but not before planting a few crosses on Indian land. The Spaniards planted one such cross at Pecos Pueblo as if staking a claim. They would eventually return and drive the stake further into the heart of the Pueblo.

A few more explorers visited Pecos, and at least one was met with hostility. Finally, the Spaniards came to the conclusion that gold was not to be had in New Mexico, but there were Indians to be converted and lands to be colonized by settlers. In 1598, Don Juan Oñate entered with settlers, livestock, and ten Franciscan friars. He immediately assigned one to Pecos, deemed to be the richest and most powerful pueblo. The first efforts of building a mission church there were thwarted when the pueblos, as a whole, resisted conversion, but the construction resumed in 1621. The hundred-and-fifty-foot-long, ninety-foot-wide Misión de Nuestra Señora de los Angeles was built south of the pueblo. It was the most imposing of missions in the province, with towers, buttresses, and great pine-log beams hauled from the mountains. Resentment continued and Pecos literally went through dozens of priests. During the Pueblo Revolt of 1680, legendarily led by Popé of Pecos, the Spaniards retreated to Mexico, and although some loyal Pecos parishioners tried to warn the priest of the conspiracy, he was murdered and the church destroyed. In a symbolic gesture, they built a forbidden *kiva* (underground ceremonial chamber) in the mission's *convento,* once sheltering the priests' quarters, corrals, stables, kitchen, garden, and dining area.

Twelve years later, Diego de Vargas reconquered New Mexico. He expected a fight at Pecos, but found that sentiments had shifted. They even helped him retake Santa Fe. On the ruins of the former mission, the Franciscans built a more discreet church, with a doubled *convento* of workshops and gardens, emphasizing the education rather than the conversion. It was, appropriately, the first mission of the Reconquest. A majority of Pecos people helped the Spanish sustain their rule until the Mexican Independence in 1821. In return, the Franciscans moderated their old zeal, abolished tribute, and the Pecos, as allies and traders, became partners in a relaxed Spanish-Pueblo community. The Hispanos, dependent upon the interim missionary of Pecos, participated in the ancient trade fairs held at Pecos, which were attended by Plains and other Pueblo tribes. Pecos became the point of entry for Anglo traders and explorers from the east.

By the 1780s, disease, Comanche raids, and migration reduced the Pecos population to less than three hundred. Long-standing internal divisions between *Kiva* traditionalists and Pueblos loyal to Cross and Crown may have contributed to the downfall of this once-powerful city-state. The New Mexico census of 1799 was the last to show more Indians than non-Indians: a hundred and fifty nine to a hundred and fifty. But the 1794 establishment of the El Vado de San Miguel grant some twenty miles downriver southeast of Pecos Pueblo, slowly siphoned off trade, settlers, and eventually the priest and the mission of Pecos, now protected from the Comanches by treaties. The large mission became only a *visita* on the route of the priest from San Miguel. With the opening of Santa Fe Trade in 1818, the port of entry shifted to San Miguel until the Santa Fe Trail resumed routes through Pecos a few years later.

With Pecos on its last legs, other settlers began chipping away at its land, leading to the establishment of the village of Cañón de Pecos. Some time after the 1700s there existed (somewhat fictitiously), the Pueblo League which, under Spanish law, gave Pueblos minimal entitlement to the lands they traditionally used. Each Pueblo was to measure one league, or five thousand *varas*, from the cross in the pueblo's mission cemetery toward all four cardinal directions. A typical pueblo grant was thus four square leagues or twenty-seven square miles or 17,350 acres. So long as Pecos had no neighbors, there was no need to measure their grant on the ground, but when land promoters began petitioning for "surplus" land ever closer to Pecos beginning in 1813, they made it their business.

Measurement for Cañón de Pecos grant (also known as the Alexander Valle grant) sufficiently lopped off the Pueblo's northern irrigable lands. This came under dispute in 1818 when the *alcalde*, or judge, of the El Vado (or Bado) grant remeasured with a wet, taut cord that was a hundred *varas* long from the edge of the Pueblo, rather than from the cross. After performing the measurement a number of times in front of witnesses, the cord snapped. It is not known how this was resolved, but the petitioners for the Los Trigos Grant south of the Pueblo, which encompassed the present headquarters of the Forked Lightning Ranch, had a Pecos man do the measuring to his satisfaction.

Pecos mission and Pueblo ruins

In 1825, the *Diputación Provincial*, the token legislature under the Mexican Constitution of 1824, opened the Pecos League to everyone, and some grants were established around the present village. Almost overnight, dozens of families settled at Cañón de Pecos (or Cañón de San Antonio del Río Pecos), with or without grants, and this constituted the beginning of the village. By 1834, the priest noted a burial in the chapel of Pecos. When I visited the town, a local woman told me she was a descendant of the Gonzales family who had been prudent to homestead their land up in the mountains. She wore a map of the Pecos area on her apron provided by the store where she worked, and that surely encompassed the land of her ancestors.

In 1838, a handful of Pecos Pueblo survivors abandoned their land in a calculated move to live among their linguistic cousins at the Towa-speaking pueblo of Jemez. They packed their gear and asked local Hispanos to take care of their church. For safekeeping, they gave the villagers their painting, *Nuestra Señora de Angeles de Porciuncula* by the eighteenth-century Mexican painter Juan Correa. It still hangs at St. Anthony's Church and to this day, the parishioners celebrate her feast day the first Sunday in August with a procession of church elders, state officials, and Jemez delegates, carrying the painting like a banner to the ruined mission. Some Pecos traditions, including the Buffalo Dance borrowed from the Plains cultures, still exist at Jemez.

The Pecos people never tried to return home, but did sell their nearly nineteen thousand acres for $4,010 to land promoters in 1872. Forty years down the road, after the grant had changed hands several times, after the ruins had almost become part of a grand hotel scheme, and after it had been purchased by a mercantile company, the Supreme Court in 1913 (*United States vs. Sandoval*) declared the Pecos wards of the state, the land grant of 1689 invalid and illegally sold, and accused the Hispanos in the village of Pecos of being squatters. The mercantile company quietly negotiated quitclaims and, after more court battles, the two hundred and fifty descendants of Pecos received compensation of $1.50 an acre in 1931. Congress, in 1958, confirmed the original grant of 1689, and although tenacious Pecos continued to appeal for more money, the 1931 compensation was declared final. The last Pecos member died in 1919, and in May of 1989 the *Albuquerque Journal* reported the death of Polito Fragua, the last descendant of Pecos. He was eighty-eight.

Pecos became no more than a curious relic, the subject of many paintings, and the object of romantic prose forwarded by journalists, letter writers, and such novelists as Willa Cather in *Death Comes for the Archbishop*. Ever since Americans began exploring and writing about New Mexico, they associated the ruins with the Aztecs, partially based on the traditions of the Pueblos who had embellished stories they had heard from the Spaniards. Tales about a culture hero named Montezuma (modeled after the Aztec Mochtezuma II, A.D. 1447-1520) were created, partly as a defense against aggressive priests and bureaucrats and, later, against nosey historians and anthropologists curious about their religious practices.

The legendary Montezuma, supposedly born at Pecos, kindled a fire in a cave near the Pueblo before his famous migration to Mexico. The sacred fire was to be kept burning in perpetuity until he returned to deliver the people from the yoke of the Spaniards. In one version, the only three people left who could perform the task were a chief, his daughter, and her betrothed. When the chief died, the young man took a brand and led the woman outside the cave. The mountain ignited and inflamed the heavens as the lovers kissed.

It didn't take long for the Pecos Pueblo to disintegrate back into the earth. Excavations of the ruins began in 1915, and one of its early archaeologists, Alfred V. Kidder, developed innovative digging and dating techniques that established the continuity of the people who had lived there from early times. He conducted the first Pecos Conference, still an important annual meeting of archaeologists, which set up classifications to identify the cultural evolution of the Southwestern peoples. His work abolished the notion that the Pueblos were related to the Aztecs, while turning public opinion against the hostile takeover of Indian lands.

The year following the final exodus of the Pecos Pueblo, 1839, a quarter million dollars of goods rumbled past the pueblo on the Santa Fe Trail (which today nearly parallels Interstate 25 from Las Vegas, NM, to Santa Fe) and commerce over the trail boomed after the Mexican War. Martin Kozlowski's Stage Stop and Tavern on what was to become the Forked Lightning Ranch served the Santa Fe Trail. The spring on his ranch, only a good day's journey from Santa Fe, was an ideal watering place, and Elena Kozlowski's fresh trout was reputedly the best on the western end of the trail. This became the state's first tourist trap for travelers who would go up and see the ruins and relax in the evening in Kozlowski's tavern and hostel. Archbishop Lamy gave Kozlowski permission to use the beautifully carved beams and wood from the mission, furthering its destruction, for fence posts and construction of his house, which is the pink territorial-style building on New Mexico Route 63 just one mile south of the ruins. The ruts of wagon wheels are still visible west of 63.

The Civil War broke out barely two years after Kozlowski bought the ranch from Johan Pizer in 1860, using his government bounty-land warrant of a hundred and sixty acres as down payment. A Polish-born immigrant, he transferred title to his American wife to avoid confiscation by the Confederacy. This may have been a prophetic move. As a 1st regiment, U.S. Dragoons veteran, he was loyal to the Union cause and opened his tavern to the Colorado Volunteers on March 25, 1862, the eve of the Battle of Glorietta Pass, an important chapter in the Civil War. When it was all over, he voiced his surprise that the soldiers had not robbed him of anything, not even a chicken.

The previous year, Confederate President Jefferson Davis had approved General Henry Hopkins Sibley's plan to invade the West, to capture fort supplies, mining resources, and California's ports and to recruit disenchanted Territorial citizens. In early 1862, Sibley moved up the Rio Grande with three thousand Fourth, Fifth, and Seventh Texas Mounted Riflemen. By that time, Colonel Edward R.S. Canby, the Union commander of New Mexico, had learned of the invasion plans and had four thousand troops at the ready.

Texan forces defeated Union troops at Valverde near Fort Craig one hundred miles south of Albuquerque on February 21, 1862. Rather than risk manpower and overspend artilleries in an attack on the fort, Sibley pressed on to Albuquerque, having no fear of being pursued by Union forces who in his view were demoralized and disorganized. But as the Battle of Valverde waged, the First Regiment of Colorado Volunteers marched to Fort Union on the Santa Fe Trail to reinforce its troops, covering four hundred miles in thirteen days. Under command of Colonel John P. Slough, they arrived at Kozlowski's Stage Stop two weeks later. What is today a gravel parking lot was then Camp Lewis to some fifteen hundred Union troops and, for months following the battle, a hospital for the wounded.

Meanwhile, Confederate Major Charles Pyron and his Fifth Texas Regiment had captured the capital of Santa Fe and had flown the Confederate flag over the Palace of the Governors on March 13. Pyron's regiment then headed up the Santa Fe Trail toward Fort Union at Apache Canyon, unaware of the Federal forces camped at Kozlowski's twelve miles to the east. A white-washed chapel with a red roof and cross in front of the door, visible from Interstate 25 at Cañoncito, is near the battlefield. This is where Mexican Governor

Manuel Armijo happened to have prepared to defend the province against the American army in 1846.

On March 26, Major John M. Chivington and a group of Colorado volunteers, on a reconnaissance mission, surprised and captured a Confederate scouting party near present-day Valencia and then ran into the main body of Pyron's Confederates, who quickly withdrew from the Union rapid fire. But as the Union calvary failed to obey orders to charge, the Confederates escaped, re-established their defenses, and destroyed a log bridge to impede Union advance. Union cavalry leaped the gap where the bridge once was, charged into the retreating Texans, and captured about seventy soldiers in a small canyon.

Both sides called a truce; the Confederates withdrew to Apache Canyon and the Union troops to Kozlowski's. The following night, Union leaders learned that the opposition had been strongly reinforced and devised a plan whereby Major Chivington's four hundred and fifty men would harass the Confederate rear from above on Glorietta Mesa and the remaining nine hundred would confront them head on in the pass under Colonel Slough's command.

On March 28, both sides advanced toward each other unaware of the other's position. They met in the middle at Pigeon's Ranch, a hostel. The battle site is today marked by a hollowed-out adobe building on the shoulders of New Mexico Route 50 sandwiched between a ridge and a hill. If I hadn't been told by townspeople where to look, I wouldn't have suspected it, although there is a historical marker to the west of the area. The ground is bermed by burials and past excavations. Congress established this as the Glorietta Unit of Pecos National Historical Park in November 1990, and it is currently closed to the public. A good display of the battle is on exhibit at the park's visitors center.

Colonel Slough's men broke rank to fill their canteens at the ranch, enabling Lieutenant Colonel Scurry's six hundred Confederates to attack before the former could reorganize. Battle lines were quickly formed across the Santa Fe Trail along Windmill Hill. Union troops positioned themselves on Sharpshooter's Ridge and Artillery Hill to face the Texans, who overtook the latter hill. From this advantage, they fired down on the Unions and drove them farther back. They charged the Federal

artillery at its new position a half mile east of Pigeon's, but were re-
pulsed. A combined total of three hundred and eighty-four were killed
and three hundred and twenty-four were wounded.

By nightfall, Colonel Slough's men retreated to Kozlowski's and
the Texans were left holding the battlefield. They had won the battle,
but although they did not know it at the time, they had lost the ob-
jective. Major Chivington's men had in the meantime attacked the
supply train. His route to the enemy rear had taken him to the eastern edge of Glorietta Mesa where he saw the lightly-guarded wagons
below. They scrambled down the mesa, burned wagons, ran off the
stock, and spiked the cannon. Scurry felt he could not continue toward Fort Union and consequently withdrew. Their retreat back to
Texas was harassed by troops from Fort Craig, Indian attacks, sick-
ness, and the harsh environment. By July, 1862, all Confederate troops
had vacated New Mexico Territory and their grandiose plans.

The ranch became a main stage stop for the Barlow, Sandersons and
Company in 1866. As for Martin Kozlowski, well, he accidently murdered a man, Jose Dolores Archuleta, in his tavern in 1878. He fired off a
shot as a scare tactic to stop an argument between Archuleta and
Kozlowski's son, Thomas. Admitting to the crime, he spent two years in
prison and $109.20 in court costs. By that time, the first train came into
Santa Fe through Rowe on February 9, 1880, thereby skirting and killing
Kozlowski's Stage Stop and the trail. He died in 1905, and the ranch
stayed in the family until about 1924 when Thomas lost it to taxes.

In 1925, John Van "Tex" Austin bought up parcels of land on the
old Pecos Pueblo Grant, including Kozlowski's, and called it the Forked
Lighting Ranch. Tex Austin was a horse of a different color. Although
born to a strict St. Louis household as Clarence Van Nostrand, he
claimed to have been raised on a cattle ranch in Victoria, Texas.
Named to the Rodeo Hall of Fame and the National Cowboy Hall of
Fame, he was a self-styled rodeo promoter and rancher, possessed of
tremendous charm and bluff. He produced the first Madison Square
Garden Rodeo in 1922 with a record prize of $25,000. Some one hun-
dred and fourteen thousand people attended his 1924 rodeo in
London's Wembly Stadium.

Tex converted the old stage stop and ranch headquarters into a trading post and hired architect John Gaw Meem to build a new ranch house on a bluff above the Pecos River. Meem was to become famous throughout the Southwest for his "Pueblo Revival" architecture, most notably on the University of New Mexico campus in Albuquerque and the Fred Harvey station houses on the railroad to California. All rooms in the rectangular house face a grassy patio, and a sculpted steer head mounted on the outside of the chimney is the crowning touch. Tex's advertising for this $125-a-week dude ranch promised romanticism, comfort, heaping meals, and pack- and chuck-wagon trips to high peaks. Charles Lindbergh, Will Rogers, and Lady Diana Manners were among the acclaimed who vacationed here.

Tex always had a plan going and he spent greenbacks as if they were leaves from a forest he owned. He reputedly had several thousand head of cattle and traveled to Chicago frequently to persuade barflies to voluntarily hop a train to New Mexico and drive cattle here and there at their own expense. Tall and lanky, Tex's cowhands did not consider him a talented cowboy, but he learned to wear a big hat and to sit in the saddle as if born to the leather. Tex could not pay off his heavy mortgage and eventually lost the ranch in bankruptcy in the early 1930s. British animal-rights groups hampered a second London rodeo and he lost $20,000. In October of 1938 Tex committed suicide.

About that time, Colonel E.E. "Buddy" Fogelson bought the Forked Lightning Ranch from an interim owner. Once again, the ranch had its larger-than-life patron, but this one was for real, having made his money in wildcatting as an oil producer in Texas. In the next few years, he increased his holding by another eight thousand acres to include the Los Trigos Grant as well as prehistoric Indian ruins and early Spanish and Mexican colonies. Fogelson made Forked Lightning his summer home and brought his bride, the actress Greer Garson, to it in 1949. The Fogelsons raised the prize-winning Gertrudis breeding stock (a shorthorn Brahman developed in Texas). Gilbert Ortiz, now a civic leader in the town of Pecos and roads-and-trails foreman for the National Park Service, signed on as foreman when he was still a kid and taught Fogelson what he knew about ranching and breeding cattle. A gleam comes to his eye when he speaks of the Fogelsons and their amiable relationship with the town.

It seems everyone was smitten. When ranger John Lolliett answered the phone at what is now the Pecos National Historical Park in the fall of 1988, the stately voice on the other end could not be mistaken. It was Greer Garson asking if she could come see the ruins that day. Mrs. Fogelson, as everyone in the village of Pecos calls her, soon arrived and as ranger John opened the car door for her, a pair of hands wearing long, black gloves presented him with a chocolate cake. Inside she gave him the price of admission for herself and her nurse, despite the wave of the ranger's hand. "Now if you did this for everyone, you wouldn't have any money," she told him. That's when he fell in love with her elegance, her gregariousness, her bright red hair. She never lost that presence that had won her the 1942 Best Actress Oscar for her role in *Mrs. Minerva*, which Winston Churchill said was worth more to the Allies than a flotilla of destroyers. That's her voice narrating the short historical video inside the visitors center.

The Fogelson generosity is famous in these parts. Buddy Fogelson quietly put some fifteen Pecos students through college. All they had to do was ask him for help and continue to demonstrate their ambition and aptitude. The couple donated several hundred acres surrounding the pueblo ruins in 1965 when it became the Pecos National Monument. (The ruins and mission themselves had been presented to the state by the School of American Research in Santa Fe via the Archdiocese of Santa Fe, which had acquired it in 1920.) It was further expanded in 1984, with donations of additional land and money for an educational building that became the Fogelson Visitor Center. In 1990, an arrangement was made for an additional 5,556 acres to be donated to the park, which included Kozlowski's and Tex Austin's old house. With this final piece, the Pecos lands and the mission's beams have come full circle.

The donation of the ranch to the park came about after the Santa Fe *Reporter* had discovered that a Florida businessman, unbeknownst to Greer Garson Fogelson, was planning to develop the ranch into a multimillion-dollar vacation spot. A widow now (Buddy had died in December, 1987), her health was failing, and a fire at her Los Angeles apartment had devastated her. She needed to sell, but the nearby town of Pecos, not wishing to see their legacy destroyed by progress, urged her to seek an alternative despite the economic benefits that might have derived from such a project. She sold the ranch to the Richard Mellon Foundation in Pittsburgh, who gave it to the National Park Service, devoid of taxpayer expense. Mrs. Fogelson used the proceeds to fund construction of a communication arts center at the College of Santa Fe, which has the state's first professional and fully-equipped movie soundstage. Greer Garson Fogelson died in April, 1996.

Gayle, an orphaned nephew of Buddy Fogelson, inherited the southern portion of the ranch that included the Los Trigos Grant. The younger Fogelson, a Dallas businessman and art dealer who had spent his summers on the ranch, sold part of his inheritance to a Norwegian fiord horse operation and the remainder to a developer, much to the consternation of the local population. Such development projects would have been a boon to the town of Pecos. But Pecos villagers, having learned the lessons of the past, prefer preservation over progress that has come too quickly.

A shining example of this near-anonymous citizenship was Octaviano Segura, who in 1934 convincingly argued the need for better schools in Pecos in "well-arranged and appropriate bouquets of rhetoric." Omar Barker, in the New Mexico Quarterly (1934), wrote, "I have never met a man of more natural refinement and yet he lived a humble life in Pecos, little known beyond a few precincts surrounding the area."

I had the pleasure of touring the Forked Lightening Ranch with John Lolliett, who was still in his woolen Union-soldier's uniform after an artillery demonstration at the park. One of the few changes Mrs. Fogelson had made was to paint architect Meem's buckskin-brown exterior an orange shade of pink, which the park is debating about restoring. To think, Gregory Peck and Charlton Heston once stood beneath the beamed ceilings in the great room and viewed the same lush river I could see through the front window. When Mrs. Fogelson turned over the house, each one of the nine bedrooms was left as if she had expected guests— right down to fresh sheets on the beds and necessities in the bathrooms. She had even stocked the kitchen and left her recipes in the drawers.

The house headquarters archaeological crews for sites on the property from all time periods. The National Park Service proposes turning the ranch house into an environmental study center where school groups can spend the night. A trail along the river would lead to Kozlowski's and to picnic tables at the Gateway Overlook, from where the ruins can be viewed. The Park Service plans to repair and stabilize Pigeon's ranch and to build a three-mile loop trail that takes in the important battle landmarks. Full development of the ranch depends on the Park Service's ability to acquire the remaining private land and the decision to move New Mexico Route 50 which now runs right through the battlefield. An overlook with exhibits at Cañoncito, where the Union troops destroyed the Confederate supply train, is also in the works.

Highway 63 heads north through the village of Pecos for twenty miles, curving through the valley past smaller villages, resorts, campgrounds, summer camps, and ranches and dead-ends at Cowles, a hunting and fishing resort established in 1900. In the past, I have spotted eagles flying the thermals over the mesa on the west side of the river. Many trails and forest roads spider-leg from here to some of New Mexico's most famous peaks and lakes: Pecos Baldy, Truchas Peak, Santa Fe Baldy, and Lake Catherine. Visitors are encouraged to stop at the ranger station for permits. Groceries, hardware, building supplies, sporting and camping outfitting, and clothing are available at Adele's Town & Country Store. We always grab a green-chili hamburger at Herrera's, which serves little rum, black forest, and carrot bundt cakes and professional-quality chocolates made in the kitchen. Renata's near Glorieta on New Mexico Route 50 serves gourmet cooking and is good if you can catch it open.

Glorieta is a historical sister village to Pecos a brief six miles away. The village, mainly a Santa Fe commuter subdivision, acquired a post office in 1880. The steeple of the Glorieta Conference Center is a familiar landmark on the north side of Interstate 25. Founded in 1935 by the Sunday School Board of the Southern Baptist Convention, it can house between thirty-eight hundred and ten thousand people on its twenty-five hundred acres for Christian-oriented events. If one follows the sign to the village of Glorieta, one will come to the post office and fire station... and little else that resembles civilization. This is how we stumbled upon the Silvertip Traders, which from the outside looks more like an outlaw's hide-out or a home to eccentrics than a shop. The old adobe is covered with sun-bleached animal skulls and chili *ristras* (ornate strings of peppers) and no less than ten lounging and roughhousing dogs.

Lorraine and Max Anderson make 1840s-style clothing so authentic that their work has appeared in such movies as *Geronimo*, *Young Guns II*, *Back to the Future III*, and western episodes of *Star Trek: The Next Generation*. I got to hold the hat the Mexican cook, Po Campo, wore in *Lonesome Dove*. Silvertip Trader is what happens when a seamstress and a silversmith/leather tooler team up with a common obsession for the historical West. She makes exquisite four-tiered broomstick skirts (four tiers disguise hips better than three), fiesta blouses, bolero jackets, and leather coats; he furnishes the silver buttons, conchas, spurs, fringe, canteens, holsters, hats, and saddlebags. The couple began making these items to trade at "rendezvous" tent gatherings of folks who like to pretend they're living in the early nineteenth century, a week at a time. (See Lincoln chapter.) As business went commercial, the Andersons sold their auto shop in Kansas and moved to Glorietta lock, stock, and barn—the dark wood of the old barn now panels the shop's interior.

Of all the towns we visited, I found Pecos-Glorietta to be the most private. One secluded inn in a beautifully restored nineteenth-century adobe hacienda rejected advertisement in this book for the reason that the owner preferred patrons who planned to stay a week or more and who had tame (or better yet, no) children. But then, he wasn't from around here.

For more information:

(Addresses are in Pecos, NM 87552)
Pecos National Historical Park, 505-757-6414
Pecos District Ranger Station, Box 429

Additional information:

Silvertip, Glorietta, NM 87535, 505-757-6957

Directions:

In northeast New Mexico exit Interstate 25 south of Raton on U.S. Route 64 or north of Springer on New Mexico Route 58, or at Springer on New Mexico Route 21 west through historic Rayado and Philmont Scout Ranch. Alternatively, drive the Enchanted Circle from Taos, following U.S. Route 64 to Cimarron via Angel Fire and Eagle Nest; or head north on New Mexico Route 522 to Questa and east on New Mexico Route 38 through Red River and Elizabethtown and connect with U.S. Route 64 at Eagle Nest east to Cimarron. Population: 1,000; elevation: 6,450; county: Colfax.

Highlights:

Cimarron Canyon State Park; Old Mill Museum; St. James Hotel; Seton Memorial Library; Philmont Scout Ranch; Philmont Museum; the old jail at Apache Ridge RV Park; Kit Carson Museum in nearby Rayado; rich history in the former lands of the Utes and Apaches; Lucien Maxwell's legendary land holdings.

CHAPTER 10

CIMARRON

Simmering Cimarron

imarron is one of the few towns in New Mexico that adver-
tises the local cemetery on its brochure. The remains of
Davy Crockett were allegedly buried here, although the
marker was stolen by someone claiming to be kin—but that's
not the source of Cimarron's notoriety. This was once the seat of the
single, largest piece of property in the western hemisphere and consequently the battlefield for a bloody land-grant war. As the former
domain of the Utes and Apaches and as a ranching and mining hub
on the Santa Fe Trail, the attraction to Cimarron gave credence to its
name, an Americanized Spanish word meaning "wild and unbroken."
The St. James Hotel alone was the crime scene of twenty-six mur-
ders, and some of the victims still haunt the place. It got to the point
that a lull in the violence was reported in the *Las Vegas Gazette*.

Cimarron is today accessible to history buffs and wilderness seekers,
and the town is still very much alive. When one breathes the fresh
ozone of a mountain rain, one doesn't think of the town's fatal past.
The other applications of the Spanish word *cimarrón* seem more appropriate. The word, first referring to West Indies slaves, also described the
indigenous rugged sheep, plums, or such jagged peaks as the nearby
"Tooth of Time." The town is located on a narrow shelf of land that
divides the great Rayado and Cimarron Valleys to the south and east
from the lofty Sangre de Cristo range rising west and north. The
Cimarron River flows through a cathedral of trees and vertical rock
formations west of town. Highway 64 parallels the river through the
narrow, twisting gorge linking motorists to the Enchanted Circle of
mountain towns. Traveling in a clockwise direction, these include: Angel
Fire, Taos, Quest, Red River, Elizabethtown (an abandoned mining

town), and Eagle Nest near well-known lakes, ski resorts, and Hispanic and Pueblo points of interest. On the plains east of the mountains are a handful of little-visited but historically rich communities like Raton, Springer, Wagon Mound, Clayton, and Vermejo Park. Cimarron makes an excellent base from which to explore the region.

For a taste of Cimarron's character, one must meet her founder and most complex citizen, Lucien Bonaparte Maxwell. Men like him in those days needed a large chunk of land just to hold them. Maxwell had inherited much of his two million acres from his father-in-law, Charles (Carlos) Beaubien and purchased the rest from Beaubien's heirs. Beaubien, a French trapper, and his partner, Guadalupe Miranda, a prosperous merchant in Taos, New Mexico, had petitioned for the land grant in 1841 with an adroit public-relations scheme to develop the area socially and economically. Upon gaining independence in 1821, Mexico had welcomed the Americans and their wagons, but twenty years later, it had become clear to Mexican Governor Manuel Armijo that they were hell-bent on taking over. A settlement poised on the edge of the plains near the Santa Fe Trail might just help Mexico keep its claim on the northernmost province. That and the fact that the entrepreneurs offered the governor a quarter-interest in the grant didn't hurt in pushing it through. He never enjoyed the full benefit of the claim, for he skipped back to Mexico when, in 1846, General Stephen Kearny led American troops into Las Vegas.

Before settling Cimarron, Lucien Maxwell and his wife, Luz, built a rambling one-story hacienda twelve miles south on the banks of the Rayado River in 1848. Rayado is Spanish for "streaked" and might have referred to the spectacularly striated cliffs not far away. Christopher "Kit" Carson, Maxwell's cohort, built his own place a few miles away. Maxwell was in his early thirties when he settled there, but he was no greenhorn. Up to this point, he had been an Indian trader and had ridden with Captain John Frémont and Carson on two expeditions out of St. Louis, once bravely confronting a band of three hundred Arapaho warriors. Born in Kaskaskia, Illinois, in 1818, he considered the West, all of it from the Mississippi to the Pacific, his home. He and Carson often put together two herds of sheep and drove them through Wyoming to California. On one such drive they lost $100,000 to highway men on the Oregon Trail, but undaunted, they did it all over again.

Maxwell's first house at Rayado has been renovated and is now the Kit Carson Museum where tours are given each day from June through August by staff in period costumes. The week Andrew and I visited in July, 1995, Rayado was officially designated a Santa Fe National Historic Trail site. After two years of research, it was confirmed that Rayado had served as a way station between Raton and Fort Union. The area will be historically restored by the National Park Service.

Maxwell built a virtual baronial hall on the banks of the Cimarron River in 1858 to catch the Santa Fe Trail traffic there. Called a mansion by contrast to other adobe huts in the area, it was actually two houses separated by a patio and furnished in heavy Victorian furniture, deep carpets, velvet drapes, gold-framed oil paintings, and a number of pianos. Maxwell lived in a sort of barbaric splendor akin to that of the nobles of England at the time of the Norman conquest. An estimated five hundred to a thousand laborers farmed the estate according to the Mexican peonage system then existing in the territory. Like the noble barbarians, he was given to whipping servants and torturing, even killing, thieves. As a reward for returning a stolen box of $8,000, he once gave a Mexican man a quarter with which to buy a rope to hang himself for not keeping the money.

But for all his cruelty, Maxwell was renowned for his generosity. He put many men in the stock business with a starter herd and a piece of land to be run on shares. In return, when he needed stock, hay, or grain to fill his contracts to nearby army posts, he'd call in his shareholders for their surplus, and it was given to him without question. He was associated in a goat and sheep ranch near Cimarron with "Buffalo Bill" Cody.

His extravagance borders on legend. Everyone in Cimarron talks about the thousands of dollars he'd leave in a cowhide trunk in his bedroom. Bedclothes were laid daily for thirty guests, invited or not. His manor house on the shaded plateau at the foot of the mighty mountains served as an asylum for overland passengers left stranded by flooding streams, and they were lavishly entertained. If they had a penchant for gambling, they could lay wagers at Maxwell's racetrack or at billiards, monte, poker, and roulette in his gaming hall. He'd wring out every last cent opposing players brought with them, and then he'd give them or lend them as much as a thousand dollars the next day. When one guest demanded paying for his keep, he charged twenty dollars, and then lit his cigar with the bill. Vainglorious, but not greedy, Maxwell charged only $24 annual rent on placer claims after gold was struck in 1866 by soldiers on the western slope of Baldy Mountain within the grant. His own mining company was estimated to make $2 million, but he was supposedly uninterested. Closer to the truth, however, he had invested a fortune in a mining venture that went bust.

By that time, Maxwell's enthusiasm as a land baron began to wane. Cimarron had become a small town and was crowding up. Kit Carson, who had moved to Taos years before, had died in 1868. The following year, Maxwell sold the grant and moved to the then-abandoned Fort Sumner. A few years earlier, Carson had herded thousands of Navajos and Apaches to the fort on the Bosque Redondo, and during the year of his death, they were released. (See Fort Sumner chapter.) Maxwell turned the officers' quarters into a house where he lived and went into a slow decline, losing money in various sheep-raising, banking, and railroading schemes. In the summer of 1875, Lucien Maxwell died from what was diagnosed as uremic poisoning. He was fifty-one and broke. There's a folksy concrete statue of him holding a rifle in the park along U.S. Route 64. The primary colors are touched up every few years.

In his wake, Maxwell left what was to be called the Colfax County War. It seems that no one owner or country had ever bothered to survey the boundaries of the Miranda and Beaubien grants. Congress had confirmed the claim in 1860 without ever sending out a survey crew, and when Maxwell later decided to sell, the General Land Office should have surveyed it under a new act of Congress. Daunted by the sheer task, the government whittled the two-million-acre grant down on paper to just under a hundred thousand acres, grandfathering in the maximum allowable grant under previous Mexican Law. Max-

Cimarron Old Jail

well proceeded as if the new survey did not exist, and through some high rollers in Colorado, sold the grant to some British plungers for $1.35 million, who in turn incorporated it as the Maxwell Land Grant and Railway Company and sold stock on the international market.

The land developers opened a sales office at Maxwell's mansion, but the threat of Indian attack and faltering gold production warded off buyers. The locals, accustomed to paying rent to Maxwell in the form of livestock or crops, could not afford to buy their own homes from the company. Miners rioted when they were thrown off their claims. In 1874, the developers withdrew their deposit and the grant was opened to homesteading, but three years later, Colfax County sold the grant to Dutch speculators. The government commissioned yet another survey, determining that the grant comprised a little more than 1.7 million acres, which was patented by the Secretary of Interior in 1879.

As gunmen continued to come to Cimarron, fifteen saloons, four hotels, a post office, and a newspaper were established. The 1875 murder of Reverend F. J. Tolby, a Methodist minister greatly opposed to the company, ignited a reaction of fatal violence. Cimarron minister Oscar P. McMains ordered the torturing of an eyewitness to Tolby's murder, leaving his body to hang from a telegraph pole. The pastor was indicted and found guilty in the fifth degree, but nothing ever came of it.

Confederate veteran Clay Allison from Tennessee played a role in the Colfax County War that isn't quite clear. One source says he shot a few men for harassing homesteaders. He had such power and following that he could easily rile up a lynching mob. One time he realized his mistake in persuading a mob to hang a man and had to get up another mob to rescue him. He sabotaged the *Cimarron News and Press* and dumped the type cases and office equipment in the river for printing something he didn't like. To top it off, he sold a stack of the previous day's paper in the bars for a quarter a copy. As if Cimarron did not have enough of its own gangsters, "Black Jack" Ketchum dropped into town between robberies. He was finally—and thoroughly—hanged in Clayton. The before-and-after pictures are on display at the Old Mill Museum as well as a fast-food burger joint in Clayton. It can be a jolt when one realizes that the cloaked object the men are posing with is no hunting trophy, but Ketchum's hulking headless body.

In 1884, the territorial governor sent in thirty-five militiamen led by Jim Masterson (Bat's brother), but a resident of nearby Raton rounded up a posse of ranchers, who bought up all the artillery in Cimarron and marched the militia to the Colorado border at gunpoint. Finally in 1887, the Supreme Court upheld the patent of 1879 and, subsequently, antigrant incidents diminished and the war fizzled out.

Ironically, the region that Beaubien and Miranda wanted to develop is now a haven from civilization. You can still hear gunfire echoing from the National Rifle Association's fifty-two-square-mile retreat near Raton or from hunters stalking the abundant game in the region. Maxwell's fiefdom has been carved into several huge ranches, a state park, a national forest and wildlife refuge, and other public and private preserves. When the ranches do sell, they sell for millions of dollars a pop.

One of the most important ranches in the area is the CS Ranch named for Charles Springer. His brother, Frank Springer, who arrived from Iowa in 1873, stubbornly represented the Maxwell Land Grant Company during the twenty-year litigation period and won the historic case in the United States Supreme Court with one of the finest land-grant arguments ever made. He was awarded the CS Ranch as legal fees, which is today operated by his descendant, Les Davis. Springer finally became president of the Land Grant Company while serving as attorney for the Atchison, Topeka & Santa Fe (formerly the St. Louis, Rocky Mt. & Pacific Railroad) for thirty years, and he developed the area's vast mining, timber, ranching, and farming enterprises. An author and a paleontologist, he helped establish Highlands University at Las Vegas and various art and archaeological museums in Santa Fe. The nearby town of Springer is named for him.

Maxwell's heirs received nothing from the estate. His great-great-grandson Moe Finley runs a boat and tackle shop on Eagle Nest Lake, which is owned by the CS Ranch. A copy of one of the land-grant maps hangs in his dining room, and he had to buy that.

Waite Phillips, of Oklahoma-based Phillips Petroleum, became interested in developing a ranch out of the old land grant in 1922. Named Philmont (as in Mount Phillips), the ranch eventually amassed more than three hundred thousand acres of mountain and plains. He built a large Spanish Mediterranean home between Rayado and Philmont (now on New Mexico Route 21), naming it the Villa Philmont, raised immense herds of Hereford cows and Corriedale sheep, developed horse and hiking trails, and built elaborate fishing and hunting cabins for his family and friends. He began donating acreage to the Boy Scouts of America, finally endowing it with his twenty-three-story Philtower Building in Tulsa. Today, twenty-five thousand Scouts, Explorers, and leaders annually descend on the three hundred miles of trails on 137,493 acres within the Philmont Scout Ranch, thereby boosting the town of Cimarron's economy. My brother camped here one summer when he was a kid, but because of a death in the family, we had to pull him out a few days early. I remember being struck by the sight of dozens of deer camouflaged in the fields around the entrance to the ranch, their dark brown eyes, ears, and antlers peaking through the plants backlit by the dawning sun. Phillips had fenced in a good portion of his acreage for a wildlife refuge.

Philmont not only operates the Kit Carson Museum at Rayado, in the summer it also offers daily guided tours of the Villa which was restored as a memorial to Phillips. Exhibits at the Philmont Museum portray the region's rich frontier heritage. The Seton Memorial Library in the same building houses the book, art, and natural-history collections of the renowned author, artist, naturalist, and first Chief Scout of the Boy Scouts of America, Ernest Thompson Seton. The library and museum are open daily from June through August and Monday through Saturday from September through May.

Maxwell's mansion on the Cimarron river in town was destroyed by fire in 1922, but an excellent scale model of the structure, built by Roy Tozier in 1906, is on exhibit in the Old Mill Museum. The museum is owned by the CS Cattle Company and administrated by Les Davis as president of the historical society. It took Maxwell and his team—a Boston-born engineer, a New York millwright, and a chief mason from Vermont—four years to build the massive stone Aztec Mill at a cost of $50,000, and it was capable of turning out three hundred barrels of flour per day. When Maxwell became an Indian Agent, he used the mill to house provisions for the Utes.

Scouts in uniform receive a discount on the two-dollar entrance fee to the Old Mill Museum. It takes time to roam through the collections and photographs on all four floors and to visit with curator Buddy Morse. (Andrew was most impressed by the two-headed calf.) Buddy, a former scout leader from Tennessee, is full of old stories like the one about how Raton near the Colorado border got to be the county seat. After the seat had been moved from Cimarron to Springer in 1882, no doubt at the request of Mr. Springer, Raton politicians stole the court records from Springer to establish themselves as the seat. When Springer protested in court, the district judge apparently allowed the records to stay where they were because possession was nine-tenths of the law. Buddy, in his rancher's get-up and sheriff's badge, is an exhibit himself, and you can buy a picture of him in the museum's shop. In the evenings, June through August, the museum sponsors chuck-wagon dinners rounded out with Western entertainment and regional history. The steak with all the fixin's is prepared the "cowboy way" in Dutch ovens over an open fire.

A sketched-out map, provided by the museum, guides visitors to buildings that have served as Scwenk's (pronounced Swink's) Gambling Hall now closed to the public, the remains of the old town plaza and town well, the Dahl Brothers' Trading Post, and the sites of Maxwell's mansion, barn, and family graves. Number two on the map has been a courthouse and a Masonic lodge, and, according to Buddy, also a bordello.

Joe Rosso's mercantile store was formerly the Barlow, Sanderson and Co. Stage Stop. Joe's been going out of business for years. When he arrived from Italy, he drove a delivery truck to Dawson. The deserted "model" coal-mining community fourteen miles northeast of Cimarron was built by Phelps Dodge after 1901 and closed in 1950. The miners were predominantly immigrants, and descendants still hold a reunion there every couple of years. Joe is in his late 80s and still plans to sell out everything to return to his homeland. You can see the old appliances and hardware on the dusty shelves through the window. If anything catches your eye, perhaps you can strike a deal with Joe. I'm told if there's a truck out front and the light is on upstairs, he's home and welcomes company.

For a tour of the old jail, stop in at the Apache Ridge RV Park. You'll know it by the large tipi that doubles as a lawnmower shed. Ira Lapp owns the property on which the jail sits, but he was out of town. His wife, Shirley, handed me a set of her keys, a flashlight, and pointed the way. Andrew helped me jiggle the key in the padlock, and we tentatively went inside the small, yet bulky stone building. Graffiti and spider webs lined the walls and wooden doors along a short corridor. We peered through the grates in the doors to view what we could within the beam and saw little more than empty rooms. "That was the creepiest place I have ever been," said Andrew once we escaped. The jail tour is a brief one.

Buddy later told us the jail, built in 1854, was last used, unofficially, in the 1960s when some thirty "hippies" came to town and began carousing and stealing from the merchants. Fred Lambert, who at age fifteen had been the youngest sheriff in New Mexico and by this time one of the last living Texas Rangers, confronted the group in front of the St. James Hotel and asked them to leave. "Says who?" they asked. Lambert nodded to the two armed cronies behind them. He stuffed them in the old jail and told them that he would unlock the doors at six the next morning and they'd better be gone by the time he finished his breakfast. No one saw them leave town.

Fred Lambert's father, Henri Lambert, built the St. James Hotel in 1880. At age twelve, he had run away from home in Nantes, France, to become chef's apprentice in the French Navy, which left him in Uruguay after he suffered an injury. A circus company brought him to the center of the Civil War. Signing on as cook in the Union Army, he became chef to General Grant who recommended him to President Lincoln. After Lincoln's death, he headed west to pan for gold. Finding this venture unprofitable and unfulfilling, he opened a saloon in Cimarron in 1873, which became the St. James Hotel. His hospitality grew in reputation, attracting the famous and the infamous.

Reopened in 1985 and now operated by the Champion family, this restored national landmark offers visitors the chance to relive the glory days of the Santa Fe Trail. The two-dollar tour guides visitors to evidence of its violent and luxurious past. The original saloon is now the dining room where Clay Allison danced on the bar, and the twenty-seven bullet holes are still visible in the tin pressed ceiling. Whenever anyone was killed here, people would say, "Lambert had a man for breakfast."

The main features of the lobby are two large paintings: one of St. James and the other of Don Diego de Vargas, the leader of the Reconquest of New Mexico in 1692. In an effort to revitalize business at the beginning of the century and to sluff off the violent reputation, the hotel's name was changed for a period to the Don Diego Tavern. In the Spanish tradition, an artist never paints a portrait of a conqueror without an accompanying portrait of a saint.

The rooms in the historic section of the hotel are named for the people who boarded there, including Pancho Griego, Bat Masterson, and Wyatt Earp. Jesse James stayed in the same room where his killer, Bob Ford, later stayed. Barnum & Bailey attraction Thumbalina stayed here with Tom Thumb. From within these two-foot walls, Cody and Annie Oakley planned the Wild West show, Zane Grey wrote chapters of *Fighting Caravans*, Governor Lew Wallace wrote parts of *Ben Hur*, and Frederic Remington sketched the hills.

The room named for Lambert's first wife, Mary, is decorated in a rose motif and gives off a ghostly scent of roses. Mary doesn't like women, for the female guests sometimes report missing make-up articles. Room number 18 has been sealed permanently due to the alleged haunt of T.J. Wright, who had been shot in the saloon while playing cards. According to tradition, a shot of Jack Daniels left in the room will be drained the next morning. The room has triggered endless national attention by such shows as *Unsolved Mysteries*.

Today, the hotel offers fifteen restored rooms decorated in priceless antiques and an additional twelve rooms in the annex. The dining room serves continental cuisine and the coffee-shop menu is also gourmet. If this isn't enough, you can assume the roles of these historic characters during the murder-mystery weekends sponsored by the hotel year-round. Contact the hotel for prices and more information.

A new wave of prosperity swept over Cimarron in 1905 and 1906 when a branch line of the AT&SF came to town. The Cimarron Townsite Company bought a tract of land on the north side of the river called New Town and sold residence lots to the homeseekers who came in with the railroad. Highway 64 running through New Town is lined with a grocery store and a few motels and cafes. Heck's Hungry Traveler makes a good bowl of red pork chili but is famous for its Cimarron Roll—get it? We have always stayed at the Cimarron Inn and RV Park which recently received a Southwestern face lift. Regional information can be found in the little yellow building in the city park bearing Maxwell's likeness on Highway 64. Antiques, gifts, T-shirts, books, coffee, ice cream, and sporting goods are sold on the north and east side of the park.

Besides the gun-point confrontation with those hippies in the sixties, there was a bank robbery in 1987. J.B. Turner, a descendent of Lucien's brother, Ferdinand Maxwell, is Cimarron's police chief, and he says they got the bank robbers right away. Nothing much by way of crime has gone on since then.

Cimarron is not without its excitement, however. In July, 1996, a rare tornado ripped through its residential and commercial districts, destroying sixty homes, the post office, car wash, and Trading Post and General Store souvenir shops. Luann Lorrence, of the Cimarron Chamber of Commerce, told me she sat straight up in bed one night after the tornado hit and asked herself if the Maxwell statue was still in the park. Scanning the images of the recent disaster, she reassured herself that, yes, the statue was still there. With federal relief denied and insurance companies stalling, the town held a barbecue on the Philmont Scout Ranch, and musicians who had been performing at a music festival in Trinidad, Colorado, that weekend came down and entertained during the fund-raiser.

For more information:

(Addresses are in Cimarron, NM 87714)
Cimarron Chamber of Commerce,
    505-376-2417, 505-376-2614, 800-700-4298
Old Mill Museum, 505-376-2827
St. James Hotel, 505-376-3664, 800-748-2694
Cimarron Inn and RV Park (chuck wagon dinner tickets),
    505-376-2268, 800-546-2244
Apache Ridge RV Park (old jail), 505-376-2406
Hecks Hungry Traveler, 505-376-2574
Cimarron Canyon State Park, 505-377-6271
Kit Carson Museum, Villa Philmont, Philmont Museum, Seton
    Library, and Philmont Scout Ranch, 505-376-2281

Directions:

From the north, exit Interstate 40 at Santa Rosa about a hundred miles west of Albuquerque and drive south forty-three miles on U.S. Route 84 to Fort Sumner in eastern New Mexico. To get to the old Fort Sumner State Monument, drive east three miles from the town of Fort Sumner on U.S. Routes 60/84 to State Road 272 and turn south four miles. Population: 1,200; elevation: 4,030; county: De Baca.

Highlights:

Lake Sumner State Park; Fort Sumner State Monument; Old Fort Museum; Billy the Kid Museum; Old Fort Days; De Baca County Courthouse Murals; Bosque Redondo Park; collectibles at the Silver Dollar; Bear Track Trading Post with Southwestern art; Sprout's Cafe; Rodeo Cafe.

CHAPTER 11

FORT SUMNER

The Murals of Fort Sumner

ort Sumner is a small agricultural town tucked into the breaks of the caprock off the *llano estacado* (staked plains) in the middle of nowhere. Thousands of Navajos and Apaches were once forced onto a nearby reservation, and Billy the Kid's grave and two museums are here. There are no swanky bed and breakfasts nor historical restaurants to otherwise entice travelers off the major highways. What's worth seeing is Fort Sumner's little-known propensity to paint murals in the most unconventional places. These dozen panoramic scenes are not only artfully done, they reveal something of the town's humanity and its attempt to come to terms with its past.

The pictorial graffiti art began in 1934 when artist Russell Vernon Hunter was commissioned under the WPA to paint three murals for the new De Baca County Courthouse in Fort Sumner. (Fort Sumner became the seat in 1917 of the newly formed De Baca County, named for Exequiel Cabeza de Baca, the second governor of New Mexico after statehood in 1912.) A graduate of the Chicago Art Institute and a New Mexican by choice, Hunter taught in New York and California art institutes and in New Mexico school systems and administered arts projects and museums both locally and nationally. Eastern New Mexico drew his talents and interests the most, and the courthouse murals reflect this passion.

The old courthouse sits atop the only hill in Fort Sumner. You can't miss the long barrel of the old World War II artillery piece adorning the courthouse lawn. Children enjoy the several steep flights of stairs that lead to the Grecian pillars framing the entrance of the red brick fortress. In the dim hallways on the second floor, the trio of aging canvases tacked to the wall are laid out geographically rather than chronologically, from the Texas line at the east end to the Pecos river at the west end. When viewers climb the staircase, they step into the middle of De Baca County's history along the Texas border.

The billowing smoke of a 1907 train framing the nostalgic phrase, "The Last Days of the Frontier," surrealistically morphs into a hand aiming a Colt revolver toward civilization. The gun was modeled after the one collected by a district judge who had moved across the border from Texas, demarcated by the XIT Ranch. Texico is shown as a cow town known for its weekly horse races, and Uncle Jack Harwell is pictured shooting antelope from the corner of his saloon. The skyline of Clovis rivals that of any major city, but that's because Hunter stacks the grain elevator, water tower, depot, and factory together like a poker hand. The words, "Welcome to Clovis," are painted backwards.

Stepping back, one sees that Hunter's collage not only mixes historical time frames but conflicts as well. At one level, the artist shows the lonely prairie as the cattlemen first discovered it, with its blazing orange sunsets and brilliant night skies. Then the railroad brings industry and commerce to the open plains and Herculean farmers begin scraping the earth and pumping water from the Ogallala Aquifer beneath the flatlands of scrubgrass and cacti. A cherub pours water on the prairie, which becomes steepled with windmills, grain silos, and oil derricks, and sectioned into barbed-wire pews. Although some of the images reveal the lawlessness of yesteryear, there is a sense of vitality and forward motion.

In marked contrast, the tenebrous mural at the other end of the hall depicts Fort Sumner's awkward beginnings as a military reservation and death field for masses of Native Americans. A river of agony runs through the scene where Indian men lay dead at the foot of cornstalks, their spirits resurrecting to blue spheres against a background of stampeding cattle. The Pecos River simultaneously expresses an ironic twist in history. On the very same grounds where the government tried to convert Apaches and Navajos to new lifeways and failed, the West's greatest land baron, Lucien Maxwell, crosses paths with legendary outlaw, Billy the Kid. This shadow across American history constitutes the beginning of the town of Fort Sumner.

The stand of cottonwoods stretching sixteen miles down the banks of the Pecos River had been a stopping place for centuries. Spanish explorer Francisco Vásquez de Coronado stopped by in 1541 (although it hasn't been proven), followed by Antonio de Espejo in 1583, Comanches in the mid 1700s, and Mexican shepherds in the 1830s, and the U.S. Army Dragoons in the 1850s. The Spaniards and Mexicans called the site the *Bosque Redondo* (round woods) and used it as a place to trade with the Comanches and Apaches.

Military reconnoiters reported the "wonderful valley with acres of subirrigated grass and an abundance of cottonwood for fuel and shelter," but passed it over as a supply fort in lieu of the more accessible Fort Union on the Santa Fe Trail. Once the Confederates had been defeated in the Battle of Glorietta (see Pecos chapter), conflicts between Western settlers and the natives to this region grew. The federal government decided to expel tribes from their sacred homelands and place them under guard.

The forced relocation began in 1862, when Colonel Christopher "Kit" Carson, under orders from Brigadier General James H. Carleton, led an army raid on the small Mescalero Apache Tribe in southern New Mexico, forcing about four hundred and fifty to march to the Bosque Redondo on the Pecos River. Colonel Carson trapped the Navajos in Canyon de Chelley in what was then part of New Mexico territory, pillaging their settlements, attacking people, burning crops, and killing livestock. Despite intense resistance, thousands of Navajo people were starved into submission and forced to march to eastern New Mexico in the winter of 1864, a distance of more than three hundred and fifty miles.

Those who survived the "Long Walk" joined their linguistic cousin and traditional enemy, the Apaches, in forced confinement on the Bosque Redondo Indian Reservation, authorized by Abraham Lincoln on January 15, 1864. His executive order set aside a block of land forty miles square (1,024,000 acres) centered on the flag post at the fort named for General Edward Vose Sumner, who had ordered the installment of a string of Indian-fighting forts across the territory.

During the "experiment," Navajos constructed the adobe buildings of the fort, dug irrigation ditches from the river, planted corn, pumpkins, beans, and wheat, along with fruit trees and cottonwoods for future firewood (many of which still stand). The Navajos themselves lived five miles north of the fort on the edge of the caprock. The Indians planted crops, dug irrigation ditches, and built houses for themselves. "The removal policy was not necessary, just, moral, or healthy, but Bosque Redondo was not a Japanese or German concentration camp, internment camp, or formal prison," said Fort Sumner historian Gregory Scott Smith. This was officially an Indian reservation, and the population here were prisoners of war, but there were no barbed-wire fences or prison bars. The Navajos were guarded by a handful of soldiers stationed at strategic locations throughout the reservation. Their orders were to stop large groups from packing up and leaving, but the men could come and go to hunt and trade.

The Navajos nevertheless began to die off from the severe living conditions caused by drought, hail, alkaline water, the scarcity of wood, cutworms invading the corn crops, and Comanche warriors raiding the livestock. No records were kept on the numbers of Navajos that lived on the reservation, but park rangers estimate about nine thousand, an estimated three thousand of which died. When you consider that the total Navajo population was only twelve thousand to fifteen thousand, a fifth to a quarter of it was lost here. "That's a higher percentage than the total fatality rate of the Civil War," said Smith.

In 1865, the Mescalero Apaches evaded their military guards and returned to their spiritual home in the White and Sacramento Mountains. In 1868, General William T. Sherman inspected the Bosque Redondo Indian Reservation and declared it unsuitable for sustaining so many Indians. He recommended that the Navajos be relocated to Indian Territory in Oklahoma, but the twelve chiefs refused, saying they wanted to return to their homelands. A peace treaty with the Navajos was signed on June 1, 1868 acknowledging their sovereignty. On the morning of June 18, 1868, a ten-mile long column left Fort Sumner for the new reservation, including 7,304 Navajos, fifteen hundred horses and mules, two thousand sheep, along with fifty army wagons, and a calvary escort.

The *Dinetah* (land of the people) straddles the New Mexico/Arizona border and is the largest reservation in the country. In February, 1971, tribal societies erected a memorial of wood and a huge boulder to honor the "Navajos who lived in exile" at *Hweeldi* (Bosque Redondo). Tom Ration, a tribal singer (medicine man) and member of the Kiiyaa'aanii clan, started a travelers shrine at the old fort, a simple grouping of river stones. It serves as a good-luck monument for Navajos and others who stop to place a twig, rock, or feather on the shrine during their travels through eastern New Mexico. The Village of Fort Sumner Chamber of Commerce co-sponsored the ceremonies and served barbecue while Navajo students sang and danced in traditional tribal dress. The following is a translation of the Navajo chant engraved in the memorial:

> *We are the Diné (people).*
> *Our endurance lies in our beliefs,*
> *prayers, chants, language and wisdom.*
> *Holding these truths, we return to our*
> *homeland within our sacred mountains.*
> *Our strength endures everlasting.*
> *In Beauty we walk,*
> *In Beauty we walk,*
> *In Beauty we walk,*
> *In Beauty we walk.*

As occurred near most military forts in the state, a civilian settlement had grown up around Fort Sumner. During the 1860s, the townspeople raised foodstuffs, furnished meat and staples, and provided amusement of various kinds for the soldiers. After the departure of the Navajos, the number of soldiers was reduced to a garrison for about a year. Fort Sumner continued as a trading post catering to trail drivers, and some small buildings were erected on the Bosque Redondo Reservation for conducting trade. The Fort and Reservation were transferred to the Department of Interior for disposition, but three hundred and twenty acres were reserved where the military cemetery was located. Lucien Maxwell, who had just sold his 1.74-million-acre

Beaubien and Miranda land grant for $1.35 million, purchased the fort buildings for $5,000 at an auction in Las Vegas, New Mexico. In 1871, he relocated some twenty-five Hispanic families from Taos to start a town. Some moved into the fort buildings, while others built houses on the forty acres of irrigated land from the reservation. He expanded the officer's quarters into a lavish twenty-room house for himself. He brought in herds of blooded Merino sheep from the East, raised brood mares, and started a weekly mail service to Las Vegas, New Mexico. Thus, he nearly duplicated the fiefdom he had created at Cimarron. (See Cimarron chapter.)

Fort Sumner was sitting pretty on the cattle trail Loving and Goodnight had established when the fort was still operating under military control. In order to meet government contracts to feed the Navajos and Apaches at the fort, Texas Panhandle rancher Oliver "Bob" Loving, the great-great-great-great uncle of my husband, David Loving, joined forces with cattle baron Charles Goodnight in 1866. Under the supervision of eighteen cowboys, they drove twenty-two hundred head of cattle through some of the most rugged and hostile territory in the West. Starting at a point on the Southern Overland Mail Trail, they swung southwest to avoid crossing Comanche territory, then cut northward through New Mexico to Colorado. Despite heavy losses to thirst, they sold a portion of the herd to the fort and the rest to a fellow cattleman in Denver at a huge profit of 8¢ a pound.

The following year, they made another drive and when they crossed the Pecos at Horsehead Crossing, Goodnight sent Loving and "One-Armed" Bill Wilson ahead to the fort to negotiate the contract with strict orders to travel by night. After two uneventful nights, they got careless and met Comanches (one source says Apaches) at the Delaware River. Loving was wounded in a running fight through tule grass. Under the cloak of darkness, Loving sent Wilson to Goodnight with a message for his wife in Texas saying that he was seriously wounded and wasn't going to make it. When Goodnight reached the spot where Wilson left Loving, a Mexican wagon train had already taken him to Fort Sumner. Goodnight hurried there, but Loving died within a few days of blood poisoning on September 25, 1887. The story served as

the basic plot for the TV miniseries, *Lonesome Dove*. Loving's marker
at Weatherford, Texas, calls him the Dean of Texas Trail Drives as
the founder of three trails. This is a brief tribute to the life of a man
whose contributions to the cattle industry have often been overshad-
owed by partner and fellow mason, Charles Goodnight. In 1908, the
Swiss farming community of Florence in southeastern New Mexico,
which was first named Vaud in 1893, changed its name to Loving to
honor the trailblazer. On Valentine's Day, dozens of letters are routed
through the post office just to be stamped with the Loving postmark.

Goodnight later controlled tens of thousands of cattle and hundreds of thousands of acres headquartered near Pueblo, Colorado. The
trail was boosted by another cattle baron, John Chisum (not to be
confused with Jesse Chisholm of the more easterly trail through Texas),
who played a role in the Lincoln County War. (See Lincoln chapter.)
He arrived from Tennessee via Paris, Texas, where his packing house
had bankrupted. Chisum established a camp thirty miles south of the
fort at Bosque Grande and with a motley gang drove six hundred
cattle to the fort over the trail blazed by Loving and Goodnight. Ob-
taining a contract for ten thousand more, he made the camp his permanent headquarters and embarked on a second drive. Between 1870
and 1881, Chisum was credited with having the largest holdings of
cattle in the world and his ranch extended from Fort Sumner to the
Texas line. The Goodnight, Loving, Chisum Trail lasted until the
recession and panic of the 1890s deflated the cattle market. By 1907,
the Santa Fe Railroad Co. had completed the Belen Cutoff, a line
connecting the main trunk along the Rio Grande in Central New
Mexico to Amarillo, Texas.

In the meantime, Maxwell made several failed attempts in the 1870s
to get the government to survey the land and to allow him to buy it.
He died in 1875 from pneumonia, bankrupt. He was buried in an
unmarked grave in the military cemetery, a fact brought to light in a
1949 issue of *The Cattleman*, which caused the Colorado State Historical Society to erect a six-foot tombstone at his grave. His epitaph
refers to his achievements in Cimarron: "By industry, good fortune
and trading, Maxwell had become the sole owner in 1864 of the larg-

est single tract of land owned by an individual in the U.S." It goes on to boast of his founding of the First National Bank in Santa Fe and investing a quarter million dollars in the Texas Pacific Railroad, which are both the reasons why he went bankrupt.

His wife, Luz Beaubien Maxwell, finally did homestead a hundred and sixty acres a mile and a half south of the old military buildings and built a large adobe home which stills stands. She later deeded this site to her daughter, Odila Maxwell Abreu. Some of the Spanish families moved near this new home, thereby founding a second Fort Sumner settlement, complete with post office and church. Luz died in 1900 and was also buried in the military cemetery.

The New England Cattle Company of Trinidad, Colorado, fought the widow's claim to have improved the land in 1883 and after winning some of the land in an auction, began to subdivide it and bring in more families who plowed up the acreage of the old reservation. When the Belen Cutoff came through, a new Fort Sumner sprang up next to the tracks eight miles to the north. The townspeople used the doors, floors, roofs of the old fort buildings, and Maxwell's original house to build the new town. (A flood in 1937 demolished what was left of the adobe walls of his house.)

With the help of the Fort Sumner Land and Canal Company, the town finally became the center of an irrigation district created by the construction of Alamogordo Dam upriver on the Pecos, growing alfalfa, melons, corn, apples, sweet potatoes, and grapes. A sister town of Sunnyside Springs was founded near it, but was later ripped up by a tornado in 1902. It is said that all told, the town of Fort Sumner had four locations. The Ocean-to-Ocean Highway, U.S. Route 60, rolled through Fort Sumner in 1917 and was paved in 1930.

Maxwell's house and family are pictured in Hunter's mural in the De Baca County Courthouse. Also memorialized is Maxwell's Navajo servant, Dellevuener (spelling questionable). Maxwell traded sheep or horses for her, rescuing her from the abusive Mexicans who had taken her from family members killed in battle. She took Maxwell's name and catered to his family's every need, but her role as Billy the Kid's surrogate mother and nursemaid when he was mortally wounded

Billy the Kid's grave in Fort Sumner military cemetery

at the fort is legendary. She died in Albuquerque around 1930 at the age of a hundred and the weight of three hundred pounds.

Billy the Kid (a.k.a. William Bonney, Kid Atrim, and Henry McCarty) is the centerpiece of one of Hunter's murals. As the story goes, he hid out at Fort Sumner sometime after the Five Day War in Lincoln in 1878. (See Lincoln chapter.) The only photograph ever taken of him was outside Beaver Smith's saloon at the fort in 1879. Sheriff Pat Garrett bartended at Beaver Smith's saloon while he worked for Pete Maxwell (Lucien's son) as a ranch hand and became acquainted with the Kid. The Kid killed a man in front of Bob Hargrove's saloon in January, 1880, and Garrett shot and killed the Kid's best friend, Tom O'Falliard (lounging next to Billy on Hunter's canvas), in front of the old post hospital on December 18, 1880. That month, Garrett captured the Kid and the remaining members of his gang, including Charlie Bowdre and Billy Wilson (pictured in the mural), in Stinking Spring just east of Fort Sumner.

The outlaw gang plus two horses for warmth were holed up in an abandoned rock house at Stinking Spring. Garrett, a former buffalo hunter in Texas and now sheriff of Lincoln County, and his posse had tracked them down before morning and had the house surrounded. At daybreak, Bowdre stepped outside and was killed. Billy tried to pull in one of the three horses tied up outside, but Garrett's bullets dropped the horse dead in the door, eliminating any further attempt to escape. Freezing bodies and craving stomachs forced Billy to surrender. He and his men were fed and taken to Old Fort Sumner, where they were bound and shackled.

In April, 1881, the Kid stood trial in Mesilla and was convicted for the 1878 murder of Sheriff William Brady in Lincoln. (See Mesilla chapter.) The Kid was moved to the Lincoln County Jail to await execution, but he escaped, murdering Sheriff Bob Olinger and a guard. He fled back to Fort Sumner and into the hands of Pat Garrett. Garrett killed him on July 14, 1881, in his bedroom at Maxwell's home.

"In the old fort cemetery (where the Kid is buried) a vagrant wind whisks across the plain, a tiny dust devil will spin for a moment madly, futilely, and is swallowed up in nothingness," waxes the brochure promoting the Billy the Kid Outlaw Gang, Inc. The gang, headquartered at the Big Red Indian Trading Post in Taiban just east of Fort Sumner on U.S. Route 60, promotes, preserves, and protects Billy the Kid and Pat Garrett history in New Mexico. For a $10 fee ($14 outside the USA), members receive a card, a colorful license plate, a newsletter when available, and a ticket to a celebration/membership meeting somewhere in New Mexico around the anniversary of his death. "Joining the club is what you do around here," said Smith.

Vital to the gang is District Court Clerk Janean Grissom. Her office is across the hall from Billy the Kid's mural in the De Baca County Courthouse. She is self-appointed docent of the murals and if she isn't on a court deadline (or even if she is), she is more than willing to give narration to some of the images. She happens to own the ranch that encompasses the Stinking Spring rock house where the Kid was captured, but she didn't know it until well after she and her husband bought the ranch. They raise prize-winning race horses there.

One of the missions of the Billy the Kid Outlaw Gang, if one reads between the lines, is to document evidence debunking tales that Brushy Bill Roberts of Hico, Texas, who died in 1950, was the Kid incognito. For one thing, he was born in 1868, eight or nine years too late to be Henry McCarty, who was born sometime in 1859. There's enough people still alive in Fort Sumner who will vouch that the Kid is buried in their cemetery. Jimmy Gonzales, a one-legged World War II vet with a broad smile, has a grandparent buried in the enclosure with Billy the Kid. Chino Silva is the grandson of Jesús Silva, Lucien Maxwell's foreman from Cimarron, and the man who wrapped the Kid and buried him.

The controversy is ongoing at the Billy the Kid Museum and gift shop on U.S. Route 60/84 two miles east of downtown Fort Sumner, which is owned and operated by Don Sweet and his wife, Lula. The issue was researched by ABC's *Prime Time Live* and NBC's *Unsolved Mysteries*, a fact that is heavily promoted by the museum. The museum holds such Kid memorabilia as the bedroom door he backed through when he was killed and a curtain swatch that hung over the window of the same bedroom, but this is only a small part of the museum. Don's parents, Jewel and Ed, opened the museum in 1952 and began collecting the more than sixty thousand items such as antique cars, wagons and buggies, a horse-drawn hearse, and items from the old fort.

The Old Fort Museum, within walking distance of the fort's visitors center, features replicas of such Billy the Kid documents as the warrant and coroner's report and signed copies of *Young Guns I* and *II* scripts portraying his life and death and promoting the Brushy Bill angle. A curio shop exists in what was once the Pink Pony bar. Apparently, the owner had a pet Gila monster who sat on the bar and drank with the customers. Although there is a charge for this small museum, you can visit the Kid's grave in the adjacent military cemetery for free, anytime day or night. The original marker, a memorial stone, and the graves of Bonney, Bowdre, and O'Falliard are protected by concrete and bars. Except for Lucien Maxwell's memorial marker and a few others, the cemetery is virtually empty.

The cemetery is empty because the eventual owner of the land around it raked it of mesquite in 1939. The gravestones were moved and piled in the corner. A lawsuit was won by the families of the deceased, but not all of the markers were restored. The very same individual, Helene Allen, donated the property encompassing the fort to the state in 1968. The park ranger said that Mrs. Allen was a widow and had her son not died in World War II, the state probably would not have received the fort. The state has since reconstructed the foundations of the fort.

Billy the Kid's tombstone was stolen in 1950 and was not to be found for twenty-six years (hence the cage and steel straps holding down the marker). It was hidden beneath a boxcar in Granbury, Texas, and recovered by the late Joe Bowlin, founder of the Old Fort Museum and the Big Red Indian Trading Post in Taiban. In a mock funeral with town and county officials as pallbearers, the marker was reset to bagpipe music. Then, it was stolen again on February 8, 1981, and recovered the following week in Huntington Beach, California. Governor Bruce King arranged for De Baca County Sheriff "Big John" McBride to fly it home. The thievery inspired the annual Billy the Kid Tombstone Race held during Old Fort Days in June. The race is the world's richest tombstone race (are there others?) with nearly $2,000 in cash prizes. Two hurdles must be scaled while carrying an eighty-pound stone during two laps of the four-lap twenty-five-yard course. Women and those over thirty-five carry a twenty-pound stone. Other events include the Wild West Shoot Out, the Pat Garrett 3-on-3 straight shooter basketball contest, Great American cow plop, sourdough-biscuit toss, cowboy camp meeting on the courthouse lawn, dances, barbecues, and parade.

Every friendly town has a bit of healthy controversy, and Fort Sumner is no exception. In this case, the friction is over Billy the Kid and the right of way to the gravesite, the authenticity of materials, the who's who of history buffs, and the ethics involved in promoting outlaws (he killed only ten men, not twenty-one). Even the *National Geographic* (September, 1993:48) reported on the rivalry, which I was told was in bad taste. "The lesson of Fort Sumner is that history can be altered," said one business woman in town.

Except for the two museums and the tongue-in-cheek events, Billy the Kid is not played up too much in the town of Fort Sumner where there are eight other murals. Bob Parsons, former Fort Sumner history teacher and author of *Living Water: Our Mid-Pecos History*, painted a set of murals on the Bowl-O-Matic Lanes building on Fourth Street in 1991. The panels represent four distinctive eras: the 1541 *entrada* of the Spanish explorers, the 1862 founding of the fort and its first settlement, the open-range era for sheep (1835) and cattle (1866), and the 1905 building of the railroad and the new townsite.

Although the murals painted by both Parsons and Hunter don't come right out and say it, the coming of the railroad effectively ended the open-range era. In his running column, "Ghosts, Black Holes and Pecos Diamonds," in the *De Baca County News*, a competent broadsheet published in Fort Sumner, Parsons described an ironic event that illustrates this conflict. Enrique Salazar, the US Land Office representative in Fort Sumner and father of twenty children, was trampled by a herd of longhorns while crossing Sumner Avenue. "It is eerie to speculate that the very symbol of the open range, the longhorn, should strike down the Land Office representative, the symbol of the homesteader intrusion that would shortly terminate that era." The incident is one of many showing that the open range was not stopped by a townsite, though the newspapers after 1905 were beginning to post notices of who controlled which range, and sheriffs were already taking down illegal "drift fences" slyly put in place as boundaries. Today, when one crosses U.S. Route 60 or 80 on foot, one runs the risk of being flattened by the steady stream of pick-ups, stock trucks, and heavy equipment noisily barreling down the highways.

The romance of the range inspired another muralist in love with eastern New Mexico. Although Kristine Cortese was born and raised in California and has studied art in New York and Boston, her parents are natives of Fort Sumner and she spent many a summer here. In 1994, at age twenty-eight she painted a panoramic sixty-by-fourteen-foot mural on the side of cousin Knox's feed store on North 4th

Street (U.S. Route 80) portraying a cattle branding she witnessed on the Newton Ranch, a memory enhanced by old photos. A forklift from the supply store served as scaffolding. She also painted a large mural of a bronc rider on the wall of Rodeo Cafe, operated by her brother, Jeff Cortese.

The mural on the face of the Zia Theater on Sumner Avenue depicts an old-time movie house with Roy Rogers and Tarzan posters on the walls, people petting dogs, and a cowboy mouthing a harmonica. It was painted by Suzanne Eldridge and Karen Steele with the help of Karen's sisters, JoJo and Samantha. The murals on Avenue C illustrate the grocery store and Sprout's Cafe, which has been at this location prior to World War II. Sprout's (the nickname of the owner's dad and previous owner) is now sandwiched in between the Billy the Kid Museum and the town's small motel district. It is famous for sourdough biscuits which I can personally endorse. There are other eating establishments in town, but if you ask a local where they eat, they'll tell you Santa Rosa, forty-three miles to the north on U.S. Route 84, or Clovis, sixty-two miles east on U.S. Route 60/84.

Fort Sumner has a couple other more recent claims to fame. The late native son Admiral William Sterling "Deak" Parsons and brother of muralist Bob Parsons completed the final assembly of Little Boy on the *Enola Gay* while en route to bombing Hiroshima. Secondly, National Aeronautics & Space Administration (NASA) and the National Scientific Balloon Facility use the Fort Sumner Industrial Air Park as a base for launching balloons for scientific research.

There are other things to do in and around Fort Sumner. The locals sometimes retreat, or even retire, at Lake Sumner State Park sixteen miles northwest of Fort Sumner. Bosque Redondo Park at the end of Real Wind Drive off U.S. Routes 60/84 is a beautiful twilight picnic spot. There's some worthwhile shopping along Fourth Street and Sumner Ave. Bob and Jean Head's Silver Dollar is a magnificent second-hand store that also sells a few antiques and collectibles. A pair of broken-in red Tony Lamas caught my eye there. Bob and Barbara Craig's Bear Track Trading Post deals in southwestern art by a "mish mash of people we know."

Next to population and altitude, promotional materials list the town's attitude in one word: friendly. That's an understatement. Barbara Craig is knowledgeable about the area and fun to talk to. The people work very hard here, she said, and when they're not running their farms, ranches, or businesses, they're attending some function at one of the town's nine churches or volunteering for a service project sponsored by any one of the twenty-five clubs and organizations. When they're not doing that, they're driving an old person to a hospital or harvesting a widow's crops or helping a rancher brand calves. They'll take in people who are low on their luck, "but you might not want to print that or we'll be taken advantage of." Though Fort Sumner has its share of drug problems, it also has sports, scholastics, and animal competitions that have taken students to Holland, Germany, Scotland, and England. She offered to let us camp on her family property near the Bosque Redondo Lake where the Scouts camp, as long as we didn't try to feed the Holstein. She bites.

For more information:

(Addresses are in Fort Sumner, NM 88119)
Lake Sumner State Park, 505-355-2451
Fort Sumner State Monument, 505-355-2573
Old Fort Museum, 505-355-2942
Billy the Kid Museum, 505-355-2380
De Baca Chamber of Commerce and Old Fort Days,
    505-355-7705 or 505-355-7393
De Baca County Courthouse Murals, 505-355-2937
Billy the Kid Outlaw Gang, 505-355-9935
Sprout's Cafe, 505-355-7278
Rodeo Cafe, 505-355-7500
Bear Track Trading Post, 505-355-2638
Silver Dollar, 505-355-2276 or 505-355-2267

SELECTED BIBLIOGRAPHY

Bolack, Tommy. *Kini-K'eel, Currents: An Electrical History of Aztec, New Mexico.* Farmington, New Mexico: Garrison Graphics, Inc., 1992.

Chilton, Lance, et al. *New Mexico: A New Guide to the Colorful State.* Albuquerque: The University of New Mexico Press, 1984.

Cleaveland, Agnes Morley. *No Life for a Lady.* Cambridge: The Riverside Press, 1941.

Frietze, Lionel Cajen. *History of La Mesilla and Her Mesilleros.* Las Cruces: i g Printing, 1995.

Gibson, A.M. *The Life and Death of Colonel Albert Jennings Fountain.* Norman: University of Oklahoma Press, 1965, 1975.

Kessel, John L. *Kiva, Cross, and Crown: the Pecos Indians and New Mexico, 1540-1840.* Albuquerque: University of New Mexico Press, 1987. Originally published: Washington: National Park Service, U.S. Department of the Interior, 1979.

Kluckhohn, Clyde. *Beyond the Rainbow.* Boston, The Christopher Publishing House, c. 1933.

Koogler, C.V., and Virginia Koogler Whitney. *Aztec: A Story of Old Aztec from the Anasazi to Statehood.* Ft. Worth: American Reference Publishing Co., 1972.

Myrick, David F. *New Mexico's Railroads: An Historical Survey.* Denver: Colorado Railroad Museum, 1970.

Neill, William. "Lucien Maxwell, Esrtwile 'Emperor' of the Southwest," *Smithsonian*, vol. 26, no. 4, July 1995.

Pearce, T.M., editor. *New Mexico Place Names: A Geographical Dictionary.* Albuquerque: The University of New Mexico Press, 1965.

Scott, Robert. *Glory, Glory, Glorietta: The Gettysburg of the West.* Boulder: Johnson Books, 1992.

Twitchell, Ralph Emerson. *The Leading Facts of New Mexican History,* Vols. III and IV. Cedar Rapids, Iowa: The Torch Press, 1917.

Weigle, Marta, and Peter White. *The Lore of New Mexico.* Albuquerque: University of New Mexico Press, 1988.

The WPA Guide to 1930s New Mexico, compiled by workers of the Writers' Program of the Work Projects Administration in the state of New Mexico; forward by Marc Simmons. Tucson: The University of Arizona Press, 1989. Originally published as *New Mexico: A Guide to a Colorful State,* in 1940, by the Coronado Cuarto Centennial Commission.

Periodicals

The Aztec Local News

De Baca County News, Fort Sumner, New Mexico

High Country Roundup, Chama, New Mexico

Indian Nations *Trading Post News,* Gallup, New Mexico

Magdalena Mountain Mail and High Country Round-Up

New Mexico Magazine, Santa Fe, New Mexico

Tsa'aszi Magazine, Ramah Navajo High School

The Six County Star, Clovis News Journal

Other Sources

The stories on Foster's, prohibition, logging, ranching, and the oil
industry are based on oral histories gathered by Chama's librarian, Margaret Palmer, and compiled in the Chama *Tattler*, a
quarterly publication distributed locally.

Ramah information is based predominantly from histories written
and provided by the Davis, Vogt, Tietjen, Merrill, and
Harrington families. Further information on Evon Zartman Vogt
provided by the National Register of Historic Places, United
States Department of the Interior, and Vogt's own essays re-
printed in *The Independent*, Gallup, New Mexico.

The Highway 53 Express Visitor Guide, 1994-95, Pine Hill, New
Mexico, provided additional information on Ramah and Zuñi.

Magdalena information from *Celebrating 100 Years of Frontier Living*;
First Edition, 1984, published by Magdalena Centennial Com-
mittee; Second Edition, 1994, published by Magdalena Old
Timers' Association, Bandar Log, Inc.

Truth or Consequences history drawn from issues of *Chaparral
Guide*, A Product of the Herald Publishing Co., Inc.; *General
History of Sierra County*; *Cultural Heritage of Sierra County*,
Quincentenary Edition; Elephant Butte Dam; Geronimo Springs
Museum Tour Guide; and *The Magnificent Magnolia*, a booklet by
Mavis Martin.

Mesilla history supplemented by the following booklets: *History of
San Albino Church on the Plaza Mesilla, New Mexico*, by Mary D.
Taylor, 1991; *Historic Walking Tour of Mesilla, NM*, by Mary De
Varse and Vesta Siemers, 1991; *La Posta Cook Book*, prepared by
Katy Camuñez Meek, 1971; *The Bells of San Albino* and bulletins
provided by the church.

Lincoln history drawn from *A Walking Tour of Old Lincoln Town*, published by the Lincoln County Historical Society; and *Old Lincoln County Pioneer Stories*, Interviews from the WPA Writer's Project, Lincoln County Historical Society Publications, 1994; and brochures provided by the Wortley Hotel, Casa de Patrón, and Ellis Store & Co.

Billy the Kid Country brochure written by Michael E. Pitel, published by the New Mexico Department of Tourism provided extensive information for many of the towns in this book.

Previous Books Published by the Author

Roads to Center Place: A Cultural Atlas of Chaco Canyon and the Anasazi. Boulder: Johnson Books, 1991.

Marietta Wetherill: Reflections on Life with the Navajos in Chaco Canyon. Boulder: Johnson Books, 1992.

Gambler Way: Indian Gaming in Mythology, History, and Archaeology in North America. Boulder: Johnson Books, 1996.

INDEX

B

BOOKS and RECIPES
Ben Hur: A Tale of the Christ
(Wallace), 102, 137
Beyond the Rainbow (Kluckhohn),
29, 36-37, 40-41
Conquest of Mexico (Prescott), 11-12
Death Comes for the Archbishop
(Cather), 116
Dutch Babies, 106
Enchiladas Verdes, 93-94
Fighting Caravans (Grey), 137
Fry Bread, 39-40
Historic Walking Tour of Mesilla, 91
Living Water: Our Mid-Pecos History
(Parsons), 153
No Life for a Lady (Cleveland), 57
Puchas, 23-24
A Zuñi Artist Looks at Frank Hamilton
Cushing (Hughte), 50

C

CAFES and CANTINAS
Big Vee's, Chama, 26
Blue Corn Restaurant, Ramah, 41
Blue Note Cafe, Truth or
Consequences, 76-77
Double Eagle, Mesilla, 92
El Patio Restaurant and Cantina,
Mesilla, 83, 89, 92
Evett's Cafe and Fountain,
Magdalena, 54-55, 63
Heck's Hungry Traveler, Cimarron, 137
Herrera's, Pecos, 124
La Posta restaurant, Mesilla,
83, 92, 93-94
Owl Bar, San Antonio, 74
Peppers, Mesilla, 92
Renata's, Glorietta, 124
Rodeo Cafe, Fort Sumner, 154
Seventh City of Gold, Zuñi, 50
Sprout's Cafe, Fort Sumner, 154
Stagecoach Cafe, Lincoln, 104

Stagecoach Cafe, Ramah, 41
Tinnie's Silver Dollar Restaurant and
Saloon, Tinnie, 104
Vera's Mexican food, Chama, 26
Whistle Stop Cafe, Chama, 26
Wortley Hotel, Lincoln, 104
CHURCHES and MISSIONS
Glorietta Conference Center,
Glorietta, 124
Our Lady of Guadalupe Church,
Zuñi, 46-47
San Albino Church, Mesilla, 89-90
St. Anthony of Padua Church,
Pecos, 111, 115-116
St. Anthony's Mission and School,
Zuñi, 47-49

F

FIESTAS and RODEOS
Anasazi Pageant, Farmington, 12-13
Annual Old Timers' Reunion,
Magdalena, 53, 64
Billy the Kid Tombstone Race,
Fort Sumner, 152
Fourth of July celebration,
Elephant Butte, 78
Miguel Hidalgo celebration,
Mesilla, 90-91
Mountain Man and Cowboy
Encampment, Ruidosa, 108
Mount Tortugas annual procession,
Tortugas, 82
Old Fort Days, Fort Sumner, 152
Old Lincoln Days, Lincoln, 97, 98, 108
Pecos Conference, Pecos, 117
Philmont Scout Ranch annual outing,
Cimarron, 133-134
Red Rock State Park rodeo, Gallup, 39
Shalako dance, Zuñi, 49
St. Anthony feast day celebration,
Pecos, 116
Truth or Consequences annual fiesta,
Truth or Consequences, 76

FORESTS, LAKES, and PARKS
   Apache Ridge RV Park, Cimarron, 135
   Bosque Redondo Park, Fort Sumner, 154
   Cibola National Forest,
      Magdalena, 63, 70
   Ralph Edwards Riverside Park, Truth or
      Consequences, 76
   Elephant Butte Lake State Park, 78, 79
   Inn of the Mountain Gods ski run,
      Mescalero, 99
   Lake Sumner State Park,
      Fort Sumner, 154
   Oliver Lee Memorial State Park,
      Hillsboro, 86
   Mount Withington and Apache Kid
      Wilderness areas, Magdalena, 63-64
   National Rifle Association retreat,
      Raton, 132
   Nutria Lake, Zuñi, 50
   Ojo Caliente Lake, Zuñi, 50
   Ramah Lake, Ramah, 31
   Rock Canyon Marina,
      Elephant Butte, 78

H
HERITAGE CENTERS. *See* MUSEUMS
and HERITAGE CENTERS
HISTORIC BUILDINGS
   Ashcroft and Bond houses,
      Ramah, 30, 33-35
   Bowl-O-Matic Lanes, Fort Sumner, 153
   De Baca County Courthouse, Fort
      Sumner, 141-143, 148, 149, 150
   Elephant Butte Dam, Elephant
      Butte, 67, 71, 72-73, 79
   El Valle Historical Society walking tour,
      Chama, 22, 23
   Evett's Cafe and Fountain,
      Magdalena, 54-55
   Forked Lightning Ranch, Pecos, 111,
      117-118, 119, 120-121, 122-124
   Charles Ilfeld Co. building,
      Magdalena, 55
   Knox's feed store, Fort Sumner, 153
   Lincoln, 97-98
   Los Ojos, La Puente, and
      Los Brazos, 23, 24

Main Street, Aztec, 5-6, 7
Old Jail, Cimarron, 131, 135-136
Post Office building, Truth or
   Consequences, 74
Ramah Trading Post, Ramah, 29, 35
Rodeo Cafe, Fort Sumner, 154
Sprout's Cafe, Fort Sumner, 154
St. James Hotel, Cimarron, 127, 136-137
Standard Number 4 branch depot,
   Magdalena, 56
Territorial plaza, Mesilla, 81, 83, 84-85,
   89-92
Villa Philmont, Cimarron, 133, 134
Zia Theater, Fort Sumner, 154
HISTORIC SITES
   Aztec Ruins, Aztec, 1, 5, 9-12
   Bosque Redondo, Fort Sumner, 2, 143-145
   Chaco Canyon, 10, 11, 12, 43
   CS Ranch, Cimarron, 133
   El Morro National Monument,
      Ramah, 38-39
   Forked Lightning Ruin,
      Pecos, 111-112, 115
   Fort Sumner Industrial Air Park,
      Fort Sumner, 154
   Magdalena Mountain, 56
   Mesa Verde, 11, 12
   Pecos Indian Pueblo,
      Pecos, 111, 112-117
   Pecos National Historical Park,
      Pecos, 119, 122, 123-124
   Pecos National Monument, Pecos, 122
   Salmon Ruins, Bloomfield, 12, 13
   Tierra Amarilla, 25
   Village of the Great Kivas ruins,
      Zuñi, 43-45
HOTELS and INNS
   Casa de Patrón, Lincoln, 105-106
   Chama Station Inn, Chama, 19-20
   Cimarron Inn and RV Park,
      Cimarron, 137
   Ellis Store and Co. Bed and Breakfast,
      Lincoln, 107-108
   Foster's Hotel, Chama, 15, 16-19, 26
   Miss Gail's Inn, Aztec, 6-7
   Happy Trails Bed and Breakfast,
      Mesilla, 94

Inn of the Mountain Gods,
  Mescalero, 99
Jones House B & B, Chama, 19, 22
Magdalena Hotel, Magdalena, 63
Mesón de Mesilla, 94
Oso Ranch and Lodge, Chama, 26
Shamrock Hotel, Chama, 19, 20-21
St. James Hotel, Cimarron, 127, 136-137
Step Back Inn, Aztec, 3, 7
Vogt Bed and Breakfast,
  Ramah, 29-30, 35-41
Western Motel, Magdalena, 55
Wortley Hotel, Lincoln, 104

L
LAKES. *See* FORESTS, LAKES, and
PARKS

M
MARKETS. *See* TRADING POSTS and
MARKETS
MINERALS. *See* OIL and MINERALS
MISSIONS. *See* CHURCHES and
MISSIONS
MOVIES, PLAYS, and THEATERS
  Anasazi, the Ancient Ones
    (French), 12-13
  The Foreigner, 13
  Foster's dinner theater, Chama, 19
  Fountain Theatre, Mesilla, 83, 88
  Lions Wilderness Park Amphitheatre,
    Farmington, 12-13
  Lonesome Dove, 146-147
  Sidetracked in Chama, 19
  Speak Easy but Dance with a Roar, 19
  Zia Theater, Fort Sumner, 154
MUSEUMS and HERITAGE CENTERS
  A:shiwi A:wan Museum and Heritage
    Center, Zuñi, 49-50
  Billy the Kid Museum, Fort Sumner, 151
  Boxcar Museum, Magdalena, 55
  Callahan's Auto Museum, Truth or
    Consequences, 76
  Kit Carson Museum, Rayado, 129, 134
  Gadsden Museum, Mesilla, 85, 87-89
  Geronimo Springs Museum,
    Truth or Consequences, 72, 75, 76

Museum of New Mexico Historic
  Center, Lincoln, 98
New Mexico Bureau of Mines museum,
  Socorro, 60
Old Fort Museum, Fort Sumner, 151, 152
Old Mill Museum, Clayton,
  132, 134-135
Philmont Museum, Cimarron, 134
Pioneer Village, Aztec, 1, 4, 6, 7-8
Seton Memorial Library, Cimarron, 134

O
OIL and MINERALS
  Baldy Mountain, Cimarron, 130, 131
  Fort Worth Spudder Drilling Rig,
    Aztec, 8-9
  Gramps Oil, Chama, 20
  Graphic-Waldo graphite mine,
    Magdalena, 60
  Helen Rae mine, 108
  Kelly Mine, Magdalena, 56, 58, 59-60
  New Mexico Bureau of Mines museum,
    Socorro, 60

P
PARKS. *See* FORESTS, LAKES, and
PARKS
PEOPLES. *See* TRIBES and PEOPLES;
WELL-KNOWN PEOPLE
PLAYS. *See* MOVIES, PLAYS, and
THEATERS

R
RECIPES. *See* BOOKS and RECIPES
RODEOS. *See* FIESTAS and RODEOS

T
THEATERS. *See* MOVIES, PLAYS, and
THEATERS
TOWNS
  Aztec, 1-13
  Chama, 15-27
  Chimayo, 92
  Cimarron, 127-139
  Elephant Butte, 79
  Engle, 71, 73
  Fort Sumner, 141-155

Glorietta, 124-125
Hillsboro, 70-71, 86
Jemez, 115, 116
Las Cruces, 84-85, 86
Lincoln, 97-109
Loving, 147
Magdalena, 53-65
Mesilla, 81-95
Monticello, 72
Pecos, 111-125
Ramah, 29-41
San Antonio, 74
Springer, 133
T or C. *See* Truth or Consequences
Tortugas, 82
Truth or Consequences, 67-79
Zuñi, 43-51
TRADING POSTS and MARKETS
Adele's Town & Country Store,
  Pecos, 111, 124
Adelina's Pasta Shop, Mesilla, 92
Bear Track Trading Post,
  Fort Sumner, 154-155
Big Red Indian Trading Post,
  Taiban, 150, 152
Black Rock Trading Company,
  Ramah, 29
Blanco Trading Post, Aztec, 13
William Bonney Gallery, Mesilla, 91-92
Cumbres Mall, Chama, 21
J. Eric Chocolatier, Mesilla, 92
Going Nuts, Mesilla, 92
Mesilla Book Center, Mesilla, 84, 91
Museum of New Mexico Historic Center
  book store, Lincoln, 98
Pueblo of Zuñi Arts and Crafts, Zuñi, 50
Ramah Navajo Weavers Association,
  Ramah, 32
The Silver Dollar, Fort Sumner, 154
Silvertip Traders, Glorietta, 125
Tierra Wools, Los Ojos, 25
Tony's Rock Shop, Magdalena, 60
Zuñi Craftsmen Cooperative
  Association, Zuñi, 50
TRAINS and TRAILS
Atchison, Topeka & Santa Fe Railroad,
  36, 57, 59, 68, 71, 137, 147

Boxcar Museum, Magdalena, 55
Denver & Rio Grande, Western
  Railroad, 4, 15, 25
Enchanted Circle, 127-128
Goodnight, Loving, Chisum
  Trail, 61, 147
Red Apple Flyer depot, Aztec, 4, 7
Santa Fe Trail, 114, 117, 129
Standard Number 4 branch depot,
  Magdalena, 56
Toltec & Cumbres Scenic Railroad,
  Chama-Antonito, 15, 19, 25-26
TRIBES and PEOPLES
Anasazi, 9-11, 38, 43-45
Apache, 2, 56, 68, 69-70, 74, 85, 99,
  130, 141, 142, 143-145, 146
Buffalo Soldiers, 70, 102-103
Comanche, 113, 114, 143, 144, 146
Mormon, 30-31, 32, 33-34, 36-37
Navajo, 1-2, 13, 30, 31-32, 37, 39-40,
  61, 130, 141, 142, 143-145, 146
Pueblo, 11, 49, 93, 111-125
Ute, 127, 134
Zuñi, 31, 32, 34, 35, 43-51, 112

W
WELL-KNOWN PEOPLE
Bean, Sam and "Judge" Roy, 83
Billy the Kid, 89, 91, 97, 98, 100-102,
  103, 105, 141, 142, 148-153
Bonney, William. *See* Billy the Kid
Boots, Sarah Mara, 12-13
Carson, Christopher "Kit," 2, 39,
  128-129, 130, 143
Cleveland, Agnes Morley, 57-58
Cody, "Buffalo Bill," 129, 137
Coronado, Francisco Vásquez de,
  44-45, 112, 143
Cortese, Kristine, 153-154
Crockett, Davy, 127
Dellevuener, 148-149
Deutich, Borin, 74
Edward, Ralph and Barbara, 75-76
Eldridge, Suzanne, 154
Espejo, Antonio de, 143
Fogelson, Colonel E.E. "Buddy," 121-122
French, Sharon Hatch, 13

Gadsden, James, 83
Garrett, Pat, 86-87, 149-150
Garson, Greer, 121, 122-123
Goodnight, Charles, 146, 147
Grey, Zane, 137
Hidalgo, Miguel, 90
Hilton, Conrad, 74
Hughte, Phil, 50
Hunter, Russell Vernon,
    141-143, 148, 149
James, Jesse, 137
Justiniani, Juan Maria "The Hermit," 89
Kluckhohn, Clyde, 29, 36-37, 40-41
Loving, Oliver "Bob," 146-147
Lummis, Charles F., 38-39
Masterson, Jim, 132
Maxwell, Lucien Bonaparte, 128-131,
    132, 134, 135, 137, 138, 142, 145-146,
    147-148
McCarty, Henry. *See* Billy the Kid
Meem, John Gaw, 121, 123

Montezuma, 116-117
Oakley, Annie, 137
Onassis, Jaqueline Kennedy, 48
Oñate, Don Juan de, 38, 45, 76, 113
Popé of Pecos, 113
Prescott, William, 11-12
Remington, Frederic, 137
Seowtewa, Alex, 43-44, 45, 47-49
Seton, Ernest Thompson, 134
Shue, Larry, 13
Smithson, James, 59
Steele, Karen, JoJo, and Samantha, 154
Thumbalina and Tom Thumb, 137
Unser, Al and Al, Jr., 26
Urbina, Simon, 88
Vargas, Don Diego de, 38, 113, 136
Villa, Pancho, 33, 76
Vogt, Evon Zartman "Easy,"
    30, 37-38, 39
Wallace, Lew, 137
Young, Brigham, Jr., 29, 30

Country Roads Press

Country Roads Press publishes books that celebrate the spirit and flavor of rural and small town America. Far from strip malls and chain stores, the heart of America may still be found among the people and places along its country roads. We invite our readers to travel these roads with us.